Getting Along:

Exploring the Jungle of Women's Relationships

Brenda Buckman

Getting Along:
Exploring the Jungle of Women's Relationships

Nancy Eichman

Gospel Advocate Company
Nashville, Tennessee

All scripture quotations, unless otherwise noted, are taken from the HOLY BIBLE: NEW INTERNATIONAL VERSION. Copyright © 1973, 1978, 1984 by International Bible Society. Used by permission of Zondervan Publishing House. All rights reserved.

Published by Gospel Advocate Co.
1006 Elm Hill Pike, Nashville, TN 37210
http://www.gospeladvocate.com

ISBN-10: 0-89225-571-4
ISBN-13: 978-0-89225-571-9

Safari Itinerary

Introduction

The Way of the Jungle

I magine yourself in a lush green jungle paradise teeming with life. The foliage of the treetops forms a leafy canopy so dense in some places that you can barely see the sun. You hear the echoing sounds of exotic birds, monkeys and other diverse wildlife filling the air. The extraordinary beauty of the flowers, ferns and other greenery almost takes your breath away.

But all is not well. As a Malayan proverb states, "Don't think there are no crocodiles because the water is calm." [1]

Danger is lurking in the undergrowth. When you least expect it, you might be attacked. You may be bitten or stung where it really hurts. You could get stuck in quicksand or hopelessly tangled up in overgrown vines. You might even fall into a deep hole you did not see.

Women live every day in a kind of jungle like that. It is not a physical place but rather the realm of woman-to-woman relationships. It can encompass the best and worst of how women treat each other. Some of these relationships are beautiful, enriching and lasting. But others can be unpleasant and, in some cases, downright hurtful. No place is immune to this kind of toxic behavior. You find it among relatives, on the school committee and in the workplace. And although we would like to think it could never happen, you might even find it between sisters in Christ in the church.

How should we as Christian women handle this dark side of our relationships? How can we be friends instead of foes with the women we meet? How can we learn the way of the jungle of women's relationships and survive?

The Bible is the ultimate relationship manual. There is no better place than God's Word to find the answers to our relationship quandaries. As we search its pages, we will find that these problems are not new to our generation. For thousands of years women have struggled to get along with each other. Although some have failed, others have risen above the pettiness of envy, jealousy, competition and gossip. We can learn from their downfalls and triumphs. They can teach us how to make our way through the jungle and emerge alive and well.

It is a jungle out there – but we can survive. In fact, we can learn to thrive in a sometimes hostile environment. Let's find the best of what the jungle has to offer. Come join me on this jungle safari!

Chapter 1

She's Meaner Than a Snake!

Perhaps it goes back to the Garden of Eden, but we think of snakes as pretty mean creatures. The devil himself masqueraded as a serpent, and most of us have not liked the slithering reptiles ever since. When we want to describe a woman who is basically horrid, we say, "She's meaner than a snake!" When you think about how deceiving, lying and conniving that original snake was, that is a pretty descriptive term!

Fortunately, we know women who are not like that. These women, whether they are our sisters in Christ, members of our family, casual acquaintances, neighbors or co-workers, take an interest in our lives and make us feel accepted and appreciated. At times we are fortunate to find friends for a lifetime who share our grief and joys as if they were born our blood sisters – and sometimes they are!

But even sisters (sometimes especially sisters) do not always get along. In fact, they occasionally have knock-down-drag-out fights. These conflicts might even deteriorate into hair pulling, kicking and screaming!

Yet it is more common to see women engage in battle of a more subtle variety called indirect aggression. This predominantly female form of warfare, along with verbal aggression, overlaps with what social psychologists call relational aggression. [1] Indirect aggression includes spreading malicious gossip, playing cruel games with others' feelings, forming exclusive cliques, divulging damaging secrets, publicly making insinuating comments, purposely withdrawing friendship, and undermining other women. Instead of women supporting each other, women often sabotage each other in a battle of wits, wounding with words and slaying with smiles. [2,3]

Although this sabotage is nothing new, indirect aggression seems to be becoming more prevalent in our society today. One American Management Association study of 1,000 women showed that 95 percent of them believed they had been undermined by other women at some point in their careers. [4] Another study found that sabotage between women during the last 10 years had increased 50 percent. [5] It is much like a jungle where you have to watch not only your step but also your back!

Although it is uncomfortable to think about and even more distressing to discuss, it is important that we as Christian women face this grim reality. We – or someone close to us – will have to deal with indirect aggression. Thus, we need to try to understand why it happens, address it and find ways to stop it.

Very Good or Horrid?

Remember the little girl in the nursery rhyme who had the little curl? "When she was good, she was very, very good. But when she was bad, she was horrid." That rhyme is a good description of women's relationships. Woman-to-woman friendships can be some of the warmest and richest of bonds. Many women find that even if they get married, they still depend on their girlfriends for emotional support and heart-to-heart communication. Women bond over sharing intimate secrets and delight in "girl talk," talking about things the way girls do.

Perhaps this ability to bond is why women are so crushed when other women hurt them. We expect other women to support us. It is terribly painful when they betray us. Because we understand other women so well, we know their vulnerabilities and what can harm them. As a psychology professor at the University of Texas at Dallas, Marion Underwood observed, "Girls very much value intimacy, which makes them excellent friends and terrible enemies. They share so much information when they are friends that they never run out of ammunition if they turn on one another." [6]

In Numbers 12, we are told about how one "very good" woman of God became "horrid" toward another woman – her sister-in-law.

Leader Among Women

Miriam was more than just the sister of Moses and Aaron. She served as a spiritual leader of the Israelite women. Many years after her death, the Lord spoke through the prophet Micah regarding Miriam's contribution as a leader among the Israelites: "I brought you up out of Egypt and redeemed you from the land of slavery, I sent Moses to lead you, also Aaron and Miriam" (Micah 6:4). God chose her to be a prophetess during that transitional period of His people's history. The Bible does not tell us exactly how or what she prophesied. We do know, however, that she led the Israelite women in praise to God after all the people walked through the Red Sea on dry land (Exodus 15:20-21). Miriam must have held a position of some leadership and influence among the women.

Years before, Miriam had bravely asked Pharaoh's daughter about providing a nurse (her mother Jochebed) for baby Moses (Exodus 2:5-10). That baby was brought up in Pharaoh's palace. Moses, as an adult, later chose to suffer with God's people. God chose him to lead them out of Egyptian bondage. Moses developed a special relationship with God that Aaron and Miriam did not possess.

Perhaps it was that "line to God" that Miriam resented. She, along with Aaron, led an attack on Moses: " 'Has the LORD spoken only through Moses?' they asked. 'Hasn't he also spoken through us?' And the LORD heard this" (Numbers 12:2). God grew so angry at their presumptuous attitude that He struck Miriam with leprosy. She was humiliated by being confined outside the camp for seven days, and the whole Israelite camp could not move until she returned.

If Miriam wanted an occasion to oppose Moses, she found it in his marriage to a Cushite. We do not know whether the wife referred to here was Zipporah or a new wife, but Scripture implies that Miriam resented her sister-in-law's Cushite background (Numbers 12:1). We do not know the exact reasons why Moses' choice was so offensive to Miriam, but we do know that Miriam's attitude was very offensive to God. Miriam was in a power struggle with Moses and at the same time was critical of his wife. This fine leader of women succumbed to the pettiness that clouded her heart. Moses' sister might have believed her power and influence among the people was at stake, so she attacked another woman – perhaps to make herself look better. The real issue was not necessarily Moses' *wife* but rather Moses' *life* as a spokesman for God. [7]

Why Do Women Do That?

Although Miriam lived thousands of years ago, she vividly illustrates why some women end up hurting each other today. Often the motivation behind indirect aggression is power – power to control, power to manipulate others, power to have more and be more, the list goes on. Because traditionally women have had little power, sometimes when they do perceive a threat, they lash out as a protective mechanism. [8] As a woman living in a male-dominated society, Miriam believed that she deserved more power and lashed out at her brother and, in the process, at his wife.

What are some other possible reasons women might treat each other badly? Low self-esteem can play a part in the passive and aggressive roles that women play. A woman may play the victim by feeling she is inferior and therefore deserves to be mistreated by other women whereas another feels she must make up for her inferiority by bullying others. Some women grow up in violent environments, and they learn to survive by treating others as they have been treated. An undercurrent of competition seems to belie other women's relationships. This competition leads to covert aggression such as betrayal, undermining and manipulation, which are often driven by feelings of fear or threat. [9]

Whether the harassment is subtle or blatant, some women can also give Christian women a hard time for their beliefs. Although claiming to offer more tolerance to diverse religious beliefs, the postmodern world is, in fact, becoming less tolerant of the Bible and Christian principles. Centuries ago, Peter understood this type of treatment well. While writing in the face of rampant persecution, he told his fellow believers, "If you are insulted because of the name of Christ, you are blessed, for the Spirit of glory and of God rests on you. If you suffer, it should not be as a murderer or thief or any other kind of criminal, or even as a meddler. However, if you suffer as a Christian, do not be ashamed, but praise God that you bear that name" (1 Peter 4:14-16).

The apostle John put it bluntly: "Do not be surprised, my brothers, if the world hates you. We know that we are children of God, and that the whole world is under the control of the evil one" (1 John 3:13; 5:19). With the whole world under the control of the evil one, it is easy to see how some women might be mean. They have given their hearts to the evil one, the devil!

The Pit of Pride and Prejudice

Miriam certainly gave her heart to the devil for a time. She tumbled into an evil pit in which many women lose themselves – the pit of pride and prejudice. Whatever Miriam's reason, her prejudice against Moses' Cushite wife caused pride to well up in her heart. Miriam became so puffed up with pride that she believed the Lord could speak through her and Aaron just as He did through Moses. Just as her heart was diseased by sin, God caused her body to be diseased by leprosy.

These twin vices – pride and prejudice – go together and mirror each other. Prejudice says, "You're worse than me." Pride says, "I'm better than you." Pride and prejudice affect so many of our relationships with other women. We often exclude others because of our differences. We form cliques because we want to be comfortable with those like us and those whom we like. Pride and prejudice cause us to draw exclusive circles around ourselves in our relationships.

Extending Our Circles

When we exclude other women and form cliques, we draw a circle that dares them to come in. We can form these circles anywhere, even in the church. Diotrephes is an example of a cliquish, circle-drawing church member. John, writing in 3 John 9-10, outlined how Diotrephes had all the marks of a total snob. He loved to be number one. He gossiped maliciously. He refused to welcome others. He even prevented others from welcoming people and put them out of the church if they did. How many women have you encountered with some or all of those qualities? Think back – have you yourself ever purposely left someone out for some reason?

We exclude others for many different reasons. The writer James gave us an example of one way we might turn up our nose at others – by judging their clothes. Clothes are important to us as women, and we often judge others too quickly by what they wear. James warned us of the elitist attitude some church members had when a poor man with shabby clothes came into the assembly. They ordered him to stand or sit on the floor by their feet, disregarding him by their action. Meanwhile the man wearing a gold ring and fine clothes was offered a good seat. James asked, "[H]ave you not discriminated among yourselves and become judges with evil thoughts?" (James 2:4).

Fortunately, not everybody agrees with W.C. Fields, who said, "I am free of all prejudices. I hate everybody equally." [10] Although we may try hard not to be prejudiced, it is a challenge to love everyone as Jesus did. The Lord is our best example of a circle extender. He tells us to welcome all kinds of people, even those who cannot pay us back socially (Luke 14:12-14). Seeing His example, how can we exclude a woman different from us in race, nationality, age, intelligence, income or ethnic group when she is the very being God has created?

We need to learn to open our circles and our arms a little wider. To adapt Edwin Markham's familiar poem "Outwitted":

> She drew a circle that shut me out,
> Excluding me by clique and clout,
> But Love and I had the will to win,
> I extended my circle to take her in. [11]

Henry David Thoreau was right when he said, "It is never too late to give up your prejudices." [12] It is never too late to find kinder, gentler ways to treat other women. We certainly do not have to be "meaner than a snake" to each other. We can even change the sometimes harsh climate in the jungle of women's relationships. In the upcoming chapters, we will explore how.

Searching Further

1. What does Micah 6:4 say about Miriam's role in Israel's history?

2. What term described Miriam in Exodus 15:20? What other important role did she play in Moses' life (2:4-10)?

3. Why did Miriam and Aaron speak against Moses? What was the real issue Miriam seemed to have with Moses?

4. How did the prejudice and pride in Miriam's heart show up in her actions? How do these two vices mirror each other?

5. Why are woman-to-woman relationships so important? What makes them so hurtful when they turn sour? In the chapter, what are some reasons why women hurt each other?

6. What is often the motivation in relational aggression? What happens when some women feel their power is threatened?

7. What are some behaviors included in relational aggression?

8. When should a Christian not be ashamed to suffer persecution?

9. How do the traits of Diotrephes described in 3 John 9-10 demonstrate how he shut others out? How do we shut others out when we form cliques?

10. Would Jesus' three close companions for several important events – Peter, James and John – be considered a clique within His disciples? Why or why not? Are a group of close friends always a clique?

Who Else?

Who else served as a prophetess in the Bible (Judges 4:4; 2 Kings 22:14; Nehemiah 6:14; Isaiah 8:1-4; Luke 2:36; Acts 21:8-9)?

Too Busy for Buddies?

As we veer in different directions in our frenzied society, it is difficult enough to keep up with our commitments to family, work and the church. How can we squeeze in friendship too? With planning and creativity, it can be done.

Find an activity you both can share – no matter how crazy it may seem. Work out in the gym or hit the bike trail. Walk your dogs together, or tag along as she walks her dog. If her children play soccer, cheer with her in the stands. Or ask her to go with you on errands or shopping. One woman accompanies a friend's nighttime rides in the car to soothe her baby to sleep!

Take a class together in aerobics, sailing, pottery, knitting or gardening. Check out offerings at local colleges, hobby shops, gardens, art and drama schools and health clubs. That means you will see each other at least an hour every week!

Set aside a nonnegotiable date. Once a month get together with friends for Ladies Night Out at a different restaurant. Or every Friday meet one friend for lunch at the park (sunny day) or at a restaurant (rainy day). One lady meets a different friend for lunch each week.

Take advantage of friends and neighbors close by whom you do not take the time to see often. Get together for muffins before work or an ice cream cone after work. Friends on different floors of the same building could plan their breaks together. Bring your dinner to your neighbor's house, cook it and eat it together. [13]

When you find a true friend, she can seem closer than your family. We need to make the time to keep that bond close. As the wise man observed, "A man of many companions may come to ruin, but there is a friend who sticks closer than a brother" (Proverbs 18:24).

Chapter 2

Me Tarzan,
You Jane

In Johnny Weissmuller's first Tarzan movie, jungle man Tarzan gets acquainted with the newly arrived "woman from civilization," Jane, on a limb outside his jungle tree house. He says his name as he points to himself, and then he repeats Jane's name as he points to her. As each repetition becomes more emphatic, he almost seems to knock Jane off his treetop perch! But there is one unmistakable observation he makes from this encounter – Tarzan is different from Jane!

Men are different from women, particularly in the way they deal with relationships. Guys usually go around in a *pack* of other guys whereas gals go around with their *pick* of their closest girlfriends. Guys often bond by *playing* (physical activities which do not require talking about themselves) whereas gals bond by *saying* (sharing intimate details). When guys are in conflict, they frequently *confront* each other to resolve the issue. Meanwhile, when two gals are angry at one another, they *confide* in another friend.[1] Guys soon *get over it* and are friends with guys they have fought with minutes before. Gals, however, often let slights and injuries fester as they repeat the incident to their girlfriends and *go through it* over and over again. You might say guys deal *direct up front,* but gals deal *indirect behind your back.*

Admittedly, these are generalizations that show women in a bad light. To be fair, studies have shown that some men also cheat, gossip and backstab others through indirect aggression as often as women do.[2] But the fact remains that women often tend to deal with other women in indirect ways rather than directly. As one lady put it, "With men, it is what it is. With women, you worry about what it is and about what it could be."[3]

Dogfights and Catfights

Female and male relational differences have been compared to cats and dogs when they are fighting over territory. Furry felines do not always swipe at their opponents. Rather they posture with the intention of intimidating. They hiss at one another, arch their backs and bare their claws and fangs. Their fur stands on end, and they growl and attempt to stare each other down. On the other hand, what do dogs do? Usually they just go for the jugular and leave the fight bloody and wounded![4]

Like dogs, men tend to be more outwardly aggressive then women. Some men in the Bible are cases in point. Cain resented Abel and his burnt offering, so Cain murdered his brother when they were alone in the field (Genesis 4:3-8). When two sons of Jacob, Simeon and Levi, were enraged at Prince Shechem's rape of their sister Dinah, they attacked the city of Shechem and exterminated all the males, looted their possessions, and carried off their women and children (Genesis 34). Abner, cousin of Saul, killed Asahel. Then Asahel's brothers, Joab and Abishai, retaliated by killing Abner (2 Samuel 2:18–3:26). Do we see a theme here?

Those were violent times, for sure, but that was not true of all men of the day. Others found room for compromise (Abram and Lot), peace-making (Isaac and his neighbors) and reconciliation (Esau and Jacob). But the fact remains that men, not women, were the principle players where aggression was concerned. Even King David, a man after God's own heart, had hands that were stained with blood. In fact, it was a woman who once prevented David from killing another man.

Beauty and the Beast

Abigail was smart as well as beautiful, but she found herself in a crisis that would stretch her ingenuity to the limit (1 Samuel 25). She heard that David was coming on a rampage because her foolish husband, Nabal, had brushed off David's request for provisions for his men. David was not asking for a handout – he and his men had protected Nabal's shepherds and herds when they were out in the field. Now David asked Nabal to share some of his bounty at sheep-shearing time. When Nabal ignored David's request, the warrior and his men were ready to kill all the males of Nabal's household. Abigail literally stepped in front of and halted the posse bent on revenge.

Abigail worked quickly. She had gathered enough bread, wine, sheep, roasted grain and raisin and fig cakes to feed David's army and loaded them on donkeys. On seeing David, she bowed to the ground and apologized for her oversight in providing for David and his men. He was grateful for her initiative in stopping his mindless aggression. He accepted her gift and told her to go home in peace.

David and Abigail exemplify the epitome of what many people often think of as femininity and masculinity. David as the sword-swinging, revenge-touting warrior stands in stark contrast to Abigail's soothing, consolatory rhetoric – he the avenger, she the peace-maker. Her apologetic speech to David is a study in tact and diplomacy. Her words of wisdom calmed his "savage" feelings of revenge.

Of course, all men are not aggressive avengers nor all women peace-making diplomats. In fact, they can be quite the opposite. Researchers are finding that previously held stereotypes of men, women and aggression do not always hold true. The real questions are how they show their aggression and why.[5] For some answers, we need to look back where it all begins – in childhood.

Sugar and Spite?

Although the nursery rhyme claims that girls are made of sugar and spice and everything nice, recent research reveals something different. In the past, social scientists believed that girls were less aggressive than boys because they were less physically confrontational. A visit to a present-day preschool can prove otherwise! Under the age of three, some girls are kicking, biting, grabbing toys and pulling hair with the roughest of the boys![6, 7]

As girls grow older, they generally develop verbal fluency earlier and more quickly than boys. In combination with that, our society discourages physical aggression in girls through socialization and cultural expectations, although their aggressive impulses do not just disappear. While boys are out punching and hitting, girls are learning to use manipulation and verbal ways of attack.[8]

In these indirect ways, girls communicate negative feelings without seeming overly aggressive.[9] For example, girls' "hornet talk" (barbed insults) and "face work" (sneering, rolling their eyes and sticking out their tongues) convey anger, dislike or dismissal of other girls.[10] This indirect aggression among girls seems to peak during the middle school years. It rears its ugly head in such tactics as gossip, intimidation, belittling, exclusion and betrayal of the girls' friends as well as their enemies. What begins as a war of words often escalates out of control.[11]

Some women grow out of this preteen behavior, but some continue to act like "mean girls" when they are adults. They form cliques at the country club, belittle committee members at work, ignore the friendly overtures of their neighbors, and even bully the preacher's wife at church functions. Their gossip takes on a renewed power because they can brutally damage a woman's reputation with a few choice words. These mean women can betray their enemies, or even their friends, if they do not act or say what the mean women want.

Assertive Abigail

Another way to describe this indirect aggression is passive-aggressive behavior. The chart on the opposite page contrasts how various approaches show up in our behavior.

In 1 Samuel, Abigail was sincerely apologetic for Nabal's lack of common courtesy, and she bowed in respect to the king. But how would you classify her behavior on the chart? She was certainly assertive in meeting David and his army face-on. Another woman might have been afraid of her mean, surly husband or of the warrior David. But Abigail seemed to be able to take on both! Would we have been as brave or resourceful? Might we have sent the servants with the gifts and hid under the bed to protect ourselves? Abigail took matters into her own hands to make things right with David (1 Samuel 25:18-19, 23-31). Meanwhile, the passive-aggressive Nabal sarcastically questioned David's identity and motives (vv. 10-11). In contrast, David acted out his anger in unmistakable aggressive mode – "Put on your swords!" (v. 13).

Behavior Characteristics

	Passive	Aggressive	Passive-Aggressive	Assertive
Use of Rights	Gives up her own	Steps on others	Sneakily steps on others	Maintains her own
Description	Doormat	Steamroller	Doormat with spikes	Pillar
Verbal Behavior	Qualifies, apologizes	Blames, accuses	Uses sarcasm indirectly	Speaks her mind openly
Non-Verbal Behavior	Averts gaze, soft voice, cowers	Stares, uses loud voice, invades others' space	Uses sideways glance and sarcastic tone, shifts limbs	Uses direct gaze, varies voice, seems balanced
Response	Flight	Fight	Hit and run	Engagement

(Adapted from *Civilized Assertiveness*, p. 44)[12]

Abigail demonstrates to us an important key in dealing with indirect aggression or even direct aggression for that matter – assertiveness. Let's look more closely at what assertiveness is and why it is the best behavior for any Christian – man or woman.

What Is Assertiveness?

Assertiveness is comfortably and confidently expressing your thoughts and feelings while still respecting others.[13] Assertiveness is an open, natural, honest and direct way of living. When we are assertive, we respect others while at the same time respecting ourselves. We consider the ideas and opinions of everyone as worthy and important because God loves and values all people. We still set limits with others because we know our own energy, time and abilities are not inexhaustible.[14] In a sense, assertiveness exemplifies "[l]ove your neighbor as yourself" (Romans 13:9).

Assertiveness encompasses a variety of actions to meet different circumstances. For example, one woman might be more assertive in dealing with a telephone solicitor but less assertive with her sister-in-law.[15] We can even choose to act aggressively or passively if the occasion calls for it. Jesus was our example in perfect assertive behavior (Mark 8:31-33; 10:13-16). Even His enemies knew He told the truth without worrying about what people thought (12:13-14). Sometimes, however, He chose to be passive (Matthew 26:47-50, 52-54; Luke 9:51-56) or aggressive (Matthew 23; John 2:13-17) when it suited His purpose.[16]

Assertiveness is a characteristic of the strong whereas indirect aggression is a weapon of the weak.[17] The threatened woman who feels she has less power resorts to indirect aggression. She chooses more covert forms of aggression to get what she wants or needs.[18]

We as Christian women, however, do not have to feel powerless. Our power comes not from who we are but *whose* we are. We do not have to rely on outward sources – prestige, influence, money, clout or position – to give us the power that really counts. Rather we can depend on an inward, dynamic, never-ending power supply to fill us up! We can feel complete in God's almighty power. "His divine power has given us everything we need for life and godliness through our knowledge of him who called us by his own glory and goodness" (2 Peter 1:3).

When we understand that we can tap the greatest power of heaven and earth through Jesus Christ, we do not have to feel weak or threatened. We can learn to be assertive instead of being aggressive, passive or passive-aggressive. Each one of us has the limitless power of God on our side. That is a comforting thought to all Christians, whether they happen to be men or women!

Searching Further

1. What are some differences mentioned in the chapter in the way men and women deal with their relationships?

2. Who are some examples of aggressive men in the Bible? Which men compromised, reconciled or made peace with others?

3. Who are some examples of aggressive women in the Bible? Who are some examples of assertive women?

4. How did Nabal live up to the meaning of his name? What did Abigail do to save her household? How did David react to Nabal's message and later to Abigail's gifts?

5. How did Abigail, David and Nabal demonstrate assertive, aggressive and passive/aggressive behaviors?

6. What are some possible factors in explaining why girls resort to indirect aggression?

7. What are some examples of "hornet talk" and "face work"? When in a girl's life do these behaviors seem to peak? What happens when girls do not outgrow these behaviors?

8. Using the chart in the chapter, what are some characteristics of passive, aggressive, passive/aggressive and assertive behavior?

9. What is assertiveness? What are some occasions when Jesus was assertive? When did He choose to be aggressive? When did He choose to be passive? How does John 10:17-18 shed light on Jesus' purpose in what He did?

10. Why is indirect aggression a weapon of the weak woman? In whom does the Christian woman's power lie?

Who Else?

Who else helped to save their people by their courage (Judges 4:4-10, 14-22; Esther 4:12-16)?

Miffed About a Tiff

Miffed, displeased, peeved, annoyed, irritated, put out – in other words, you are upset! Your friend offended you, and you are still fuming. It might have been a little thing to her, but it has really bothered you. As you think about it more, this could be the end of your friendship!

But wait – take some time to cool down. Was your friend's offense enough to call it quits? Is it worth talking about with her? Not every situation like this requires a heart-to-heart talk. If you think about it, perhaps your foul temper and super-sensitive mood at the time were more to blame. Perhaps after reflection and time, you will see the matter should just be forgotten.[19]

That is just the advice the wise man Solomon gives us: "He who covers over an offense promotes love, but whoever repeats the matter separates close friends" (Proverbs 17:9). Note the second part of that verse. The best way to make matters worse is to repeat her transgression to others. It is better to take a two-part approach to small offenses: (1) Cover it, meaning forgive and do not hold it against her, and (2) do not broadcast her fault to others.

But what do we often do? We hold a grudge, and then we let everyone know why! The wrongdoing grows with each repetition; and after everyone adds her comments, the offense becomes a crime indeed. Then the friend wonders what she did that was so terrible.

If love drives our relationships, then it will find a way to forgive the slights and tiffs that come (Proverbs 10:12). Peter echoed this sentiment: "Above all, love each other deeply, because love covers over a multitude of sins" (1 Peter 4:8).

Chapter 3

Monkey See, Monkey Do

O f all the animals of the jungle, monkeys are some of the most fascinating. For example, if you give a monkey a parasol or a stocking, what will she do? Probably she will open up the parasol and pull on the stocking. She will act just as if she were mimicking a human's actions. Although psychologists differ on explanations for this behavior, it appears to us to be a case of monkey see, monkey do.[1]

Some people act like monkeys! They do just what they see other people do. It does not matter how ridiculous or stupid or evil it is; they just do it. The Bible tells us of a daughter who followed her mother's lead to commit evil. It was a deadly case of monkey see, monkey do.

An Unhappy Birthday Party

Women today look for unique and unusual entertainment ideas for birthday parties for their families. They might plan a huge surprise or rent a limousine for the night. They might even get a little wild and crazy. But few stoop to the moral depths that Herodias reached on her husband Herod's birthday (Mark 6:14-29).

Herodias had been married to Philip, Herod's brother, but Herod took Philip's wife for his own. The affair of Herod and Herodias was so well known that John the Baptist boldly denounced them for violating the Jewish Law (Leviticus 18:16; 20:21).[2]

Herodias did not like John telling her she was living in sin. She wanted to kill John. Herod feared the people's reaction to such an act because they considered John a prophet. Instead Herod threw him into prison. Strangely, although John the Baptist puzzled him, Herod liked to listen to the prophet preach (Matthew 14:3-5; Mark 6:17-20).

Just like a viper, Herodias was ready to strike, and her opportunity finally came. At Herod's birthday party, Salome, the daughter of Herodias and Philip, danced before Herod and his military commanders, high officials, and the leading men of Galilee. Herod was so enthralled with her performance that he promised her up to half the kingdom. Probably he was drunk when he made this offer, for as a vassal of the Roman government, he really did not have the authority to offer her any part of the kingdom.[3] But because he had made an oath before such an audience, he had to carry through with her request.

With such an overwhelming offer, Salome asked her mother what she should ask for. Maybe she was too young to decide, or perhaps she just wanted her mother's input. Herodias told her to ask for the head of John the Baptist. Herod, although genuinely distressed at her answer, nevertheless ordered John's head to be brought just as Salome had asked – on a platter, a grisly centerpiece for a birthday feast!

A Mother's Evil Influence

Whether Salome felt constrained to follow her mother's directive or willingly played a part in her devious plan, she was definitely influenced by Herodias. Her mother's evil influence can be seen in several ways:

• **Marriage**. Salome and Herodias became intricately entangled in the matrimonial web of Herod's family. Historians tell us that Salome married Philip the Tetrarch (a different Philip from her father), who at the same time was her uncle and great uncle! This Philip is mentioned with Herod in Luke 3:1. She followed the course of her mother, Herodias, who first married her uncle Philip and later another uncle (and brother-in-law) Herod! No wonder John the Baptist was so vocal in denouncing this family's relational intrigue![4]

• **Morality**. Salome discarded all appearance of decency as she danced alone before the men at Herod's party. Such performances were vulgar pantomimes with sexual connotations, usually performed by prostitutes.[5] Even if Salome was a young girl of 12 or 14, as some commentators suggest, virgins at that age could be married in Jewish Palestine. Certainly, men in the audience were no doubt pleased with what she provided. But Herodias allowed and perhaps even encouraged her own daughter to go in alone to dance![6, 7]

• **Manipulation**. We do not know how much Salome knew of her mother's hatred for John the Baptist and desire to kill him. But we do know Salome seemed willing to carry out her mother's request. "*At once* the girl *hurried* in to the king with the request: 'I want you to give me *right now* the head of John the Baptist on a platter.' ... an executioner ... presented it to the girl, and she gave it to her mother" (Mark 6:25, 27-28, author's emphasis). If she were younger, it makes it all the more tragic that a young girl could be caught up in her mother's foul scheme.

The Mother-Daughter Relationship

Herodias and Salome vividly demonstrate how our mothers and mother figures can influence us as daughters. Whether she was a young girl or young adult, Salome was shaped by her mother's wicked actions and words. Salome learned about aggression and cruelty firsthand from her mother. We can only imagine how much Herodias affected her daughter for evil during her lifetime. Mothers (and later sisters, if we have them) teach us many lessons on relating to other women. Speaking of mothers and sisters, author Susan Shapiro Barash points out: "They teach us to envy and compete, to support and nurture, or a bit of both. And whether we embrace or reject their lessons, we often spend a lifetime coming to terms with them."[8]

For most girls, the mother-daughter bond is the first and strongest bond they will experience with another female.[9] This is a loaded relationship. It can be full of complicated and conflicting feelings of love, resentment, worry, need, anger and envy.[10] This relationship can make a tremendous difference in how the daughter relates to other girls and how she sees herself. The way mothers and daughters interact can impact how they connect with women throughout their lives.[11]

Striking a Balance

Seeing how strong that initial mother-daughter bond can be, it is sad to see that some women today feel they must emotionally pull away and stay away from their mothers. They think they have to permanently break away to be independent and strong. Afterward these daughters find they miss the support their mothers could provide.[12] Our mothers may untie the apron strings, but it does not mean we cannot come back and visit the kitchen!

Fortunately, many women are seeing that they need to develop closer-knit relationships with their mothers and daughters. They are discovering that they need each other, even after daughters become adults and leave home. The key to such a relationship is a balance in independence between smothering each other in over-attachment and abandoning one another in total separation. Daughters can feel stronger because of their mothers' support. Mothers can be there for their daughters without being made to feel they are intruding.[13] Each can find real blessings through their bond together.

Cementing the Bond

In our busy lifestyles, making time to strengthen our mother-daughter bonds is not easy, but there are some ways we can try:

• **Find ways to connect.** Whether we are out of town or out of touch, we need to discover activities of interest that we can enjoy together. We could take in a movie or enjoy an afternoon of shopping. Time traveling in the car provides precious opportunities to talk. Eating out together provides just-the-two-of-us time that we do not always have with the family at home. Who doesn't love a funny or sentimental card or goodies delivered to her door? Even with the convenience of technology, an aged mother still enjoys getting "snail mail" in the mailbox from her adult daughter. Above all, we can be generous with hugs to let her know she is loved![14]

• **Mend the rifts**. At times mothers and daughters have misunderstandings. Sometimes teenage daughters want to push their mothers away at a crucial time in their lives. Sometimes mothers are hypercritical of their adult daughters. Pray that we can keep talking even when we do not always agree and keep involved in each other's lives even when we resist. If there is a rift between us, we need to try to talk about the problem. Sometimes a letter between a mother and daughter can offer an effective way to communicate if face-to-face conversation is difficult. We need to be humble and willing to forgive, as well as ask forgiveness for any wrongdoing on our part (Ephesians 4:32).

• **Make her a priority.** Author Mary Farrar reflects on the special relationship she had with her own mother:

"We often talked for hours, debating and discussing the issues of life. She was always honest, open, and willing to listen at the drop of a hat. She mentored me by listening as often to my heart as to my words. I never went through a struggle that Mom did not sense it and offer wise input and encouragement. Most importantly, Mom mentored me by living in the Scriptures herself. … When life was unclear, Mom always seemed to know where to go in Scriptures to meet and address my needs. She had a firm grip of the teachings of Scripture when I most needed to hear them."[15]

What an impact that mother made on her daughter! This mother-daughter relationship seems rare but certainly worth striving for. This daughter's life will always bear the loving imprint of her mother's touch and guidance because her mother made her a priority.

Although we are all daughters, we might not be blessed with such a loving relationship with our mother. In fact, a close bond might not even be possible. But God calls us to make the best of that relationship. Sometimes we will have to be the one to take the first step to make it better. One thing is certain – we will never know the richness of relationship we could enjoy until we try.

What Will They See?

Many of us have opportunities to be a mother to young girls who do not have a mother in their lives. You might be the mother figure whom they could look up to. It might be a neighborhood child or a teen in your class. It could be one of the girls on your team or in your troop. Always be aware that young eyes are looking to you as an example. In a real sense, monkey see, monkey do!

Nothing speaks louder than our lives. What are we modeling to those younger girls who will imitate what we do? Do they overhear us bad-mouth someone in private and then treat her sweetly to her face? Do they catch us rolling our eyes when we see someone dress differently than we do? Do they hear us whispering when we see a woman who has a bad reputation walk by? Do they hear us say we are not angry after a conflict when we are visibly upset?

Genuine behavior starts with us as Christian ladies. If we are phony, we will eventually show up like a counterfeit dollar. We need to strive toward an authentic life as we relate to other women. Only then can younger women see the best of what real relationships between women can be.

Let's ask ourselves: How are we as mothers and/or mother figures touching the young ladies in our sphere? What kind of examples are we demonstrating in getting along with other women? Are we demonstrating how to cultivate genuine friendships with others? What can we do to show them how to create healthy female relationships?

Whether we are a mother or a daughter or mother figure, we just need to begin. We can make an eternal difference in each other's lives – one relationship at a time.

Searching Further

1. Who was the first husband of Herodias? How was Herod, her second husband, related to her first husband? How did her second mariage violate the Jewish law (Leviticus 18:16; 20:21)?

2. Why did Herodias want to kill John the Baptist? Why was Herod resistant to having him killed? What did he do instead? Why did he eventually order John's death

3. What generous offer did Herod make Salome for her dancing? Did he have the authority to make such an offer? Why? What did she ask for instead?

4. Why do you think Salome seemed so eager to carry out Herodias' request? Is it possible that she wanted to please her mother so badly she was willing to have John killed? Why do women sometimes go to extremes for their mothers' approval?

5. What similarities exist in the marriage partners of Herodias and Salome?

6. What profession of women usually danced solo for a man's party and why?

7. Why is the mother/daughter relationship so crucial to the success of future women-to-women relationships? Why is balance in independence and attachment so important between mothers and daughters?

8. What are some ways to strengthen the mother/daughter bond?

9. How can we as mother figures model healthy relationships to younger girls and women?

10. What women in the Bible might have served as mother figures for other women? Why might they have served in this role? How were they shown respect and honor (Genesis 24:59; 35:8; Ruth 1:16-18; Luke 1:39-56)?

Who Else?

Who else offered the same generous offer of up to half the kingdom as Herod did to Salome (Esther 5:3, 6; 7:2)?

Safari Savvy
Loosening the Ties That Bind

Mothers and daughters are not the only ones who at times can hang on too tightly to each other. Friends can be like that too. They can possessively demand too much of your time and attention. They can be overly dependent on you. As Victoria Billings quips, "Constant togetherness is fine – but only for Siamese twins."[16]

Solomon warned against this one-sided monopoly of friendship: "Seldom set foot in your neighbor's house – too much of you, and he will hate you" (Proverbs 25:17).

It might help you to understand why this friend acts as if you are her last friend on earth. Maybe (in her mind) you are! Or maybe she has found in you someone she really admires whom she does not want to lose. Perhaps she feels accepted by you and is afraid to venture forth.

But venture forth is what she needs to do. Introducing her to others can help her expand her base of friends. She may be less likely to get jealous of your friends if she makes some of her own. She may enjoy attending worship with you and meeting other Christians who would be genuinely interested in her. Getting involved in service organizations will help her get occupied in good causes greater than herself.

If your friend will not give you any space, you need to set some boundaries. You need a variety of friendships as well as time by yourself. Sometimes we need to loosen the ties that bind us. As Jane McWhorter points out, "The ropes binding friendship should be tight enough to hold it together but flexible enough to allow for space in the relationship."[17]

Chapter 4

Don't Leave Home
Without It

Any adventurer heading for the jungle has an array of things she cannot do without. She must pack her medicines for warding off malaria. She has to slather on insect repellent or she will be eaten alive. Of course, her backpack is not complete without safe drinking water in plastic bottles. Likewise, any Christian woman venturing into the jungle of female relationships must bring something she cannot do without to survive – kindness.

Kindness is far too underrated these days. Have you ever wondered why we have organized crime but "random acts of kindness"? It often seems the norm on the street (or in the jungle) is to get where you are going and stampede over anyone who stands in the way!

That is why it is so refreshing to meet someone who demonstrates the simple art of kindness. It is a special treat to find it in a young girl. If we travel back a few thousand years, we can meet such a young lady.

A Captive Who Freed Her Master

A young girl was at the wrong place at the wrong time (2 Kings 5:2). At least it seemed that way. Marauding bands from Aram (Syria) swept down on Israel like locusts on a fertile green field.[1] These raiders captured the Israelites and forced them, including this little girl, into slavery. She was made a servant to the wife of Naaman, a valiant commander in the army of the king of Aram.

We do not know this young girl's age or background or even her name. Even if she were treated well in Naaman's house, what about the other members of her family? Did her parents and grandparents survive the onslaught of those raiding bands? If she had siblings, were they in a worse predicament than she? She most likely would have had cause to be bitter and resent her captors.

Amazingly, this little girl wanted to do good to her enemies. She could have been absorbed in herself and her problems, but instead she acknowledged Naaman's problem – his serious skin disease – to her mistress. It is truly possible Naaman's wife was drained by her husband's problem and felt helpless to do anything about it. Perhaps they had tried to find relief for him with no results. This little Israelite maid filled her mistress with renewed hope.

This young girl could have said nothing and held some life-changing knowledge to herself. Instead she shared with Naaman's wife the good news – the Israelite prophet Elisha could cure Naaman's disease! She cared enough to tell her mistress, "If only my master would see the prophet who is in Samaria! He would cure him of his leprosy" (2 Kings 5:3). Naaman's wife thought enough of her little maid to listen. Few gifts would have meant more to Naaman and his wife than his healing. That little girl, the captive, gave Naaman the hope of freedom from his disease – all because she had a tender, kind heart!

Does Being Kind Come Naturally?

Did kindness such as that demonstrated by this young girl come naturally? Are we born with it? In his letter to Titus, Paul told the young preacher to teach the older women to teach the younger women, among other good things, "to be kind" (Titus 2:5). It is interesting that he would highlight kindness specifically as one of the qualities that younger women should be taught. He implies kindness did not come naturally and that it comes with growing up. Kindness is intentionally showing goodness and mercy to someone else, and we often have to stretch beyond ourselves.

How do you think those older women taught kindness? Would they have held "Kindness 101" classes? Today, classes in schools extol virtues and their applications, but these older women more likely lived lives of kindness before their "students." They took food to a grieving widow, welcomed a shy newcomer to their town, encouraged a newlywed or young mother in her new phase of life, and defended a mistreated stranger. These acts of kindness translate over thousands of years to us today and are just as appreciated and needed as they were then.

When Do We Start?

So when should we start teaching kindness? We cannot start too early. Little ones are great mimics, and they watch us closely. Even preschoolers can learn from our example to start sharing and being kind to others.

Unfortunately, preschoolers can also be mean! A Brigham Young University study showed that girls as young as 4 or 5 can use sophisticated ways to hurt each other. Researchers found that they exclude others and threaten to withdraw their friendship. These "mini-meanies" use specific relational aggressive tactics such as refusing to listen (even covering their ears); threatening not to play unless a playmate meets certain demands or needs; refusing another girl's request to play with a group; and demanding their friends not play with a certain child. By treating others badly, they feel they are boosting their own social status among their peers. The researchers were familiar with adolescent relational aggression, but they found it disturbing that some little girls have figured out they can hurt others to their own advantage. [2]

If this negative behavior is not checked, it can become the norm as these little girls grow up. That is why it is imperative that we start early to teach kindness and consideration for others. The good news is that some young people seem to be learning what kindness is all about!

For example, 10-year-old Shelby Sullivan from Nashville, Tenn., decided to have a different kind of birthday party. Instead of birthday gifts for herself, she asked her friends to buy toothpaste, shampoo and small toys to be assembled in gift boxes to send to needy children in Third World countries. At the party, the guests had fun assembling the boxes to take to Healing Hands International (www.hhi.org), but more importantly they learned about being kind to others. [3]

Another young lady, Victoria Calton, a 14-year-old from a Nashville-area high school, set a goal for herself to fill 60 boxes to send to needy children. She asked 50 friends to bring items, and they assembled 70 boxes for children in Honduras through Healing Hands International. [4] Both these young ladies will be blessed by their kindness to others. "It is more blessed to give than to receive" (Acts 20:35).

Do You Have What It Takes?

If we are ever to survive in the women's relationship jungle, we must take kindness with us. But kindness requires something of us. Do we have what it takes? Some characters in the Bible knew how to demonstrate kindness in their lives.

• **Be kind when you are mistreated.** At the sudden sight of his brothers in Egypt, Joseph could have written them off as scumbags for the way they had treated him. Instead, he made himself known to them and showed them kindness. He provided a home for them in fertile Goshen and made it clear that he had forgiven them (Genesis 50:19-21).

Joseph's example shows us the real meaning of kindness through forgiveness. When someone treats us badly, we are tempted to retaliate. After all, we reason, they deserve it. But we are called to act on a higher plane. As Peter reminded us: "Finally, all of you, live in harmony with one another; be sympathetic, love as brothers, be compassionate and humble. Do not repay evil with evil or insult with insult, but with blessing, because to this you were called so that you may inherit a blessing" (1 Peter 3:8-9).

• **Be kind even if you have other plans**. We do not know what plans the Good Samaritan had when he journeyed along the Jericho Road, but they probably did not include a half-dead man lying beside the road! The Samaritan's response was unexpected and extraordinary. The effort he put forth was amazing – bandaging the injured man's wounds, pouring on oil and wine, loading him on his own donkey, paying for his overnight stay at the inn, personally caring for him, and paying for his care after he left (Luke 10:33-35). He did all this for someone he probably did not know and would not see again.

As we travel life's road, we will meet unexpected needs that cry for our attention. Will our busy lifestyles crowd out our efforts to be kind? We might be too flustered, frazzled and frustrated for kindness to easily fit into our agenda. But won't it be worth the effort to see the joy or relief on someone's face as she accepts our simple expression of kindness – even if it was not in our plans? Solomon reminds us, "An anxious heart weighs a man down, but a kind word cheers him up" (Proverbs 12:25).

• **Be kind on the spur of the moment.** Young Moses could be a man of action – a real spontaneous kind of guy. When shepherds attempted to drive Ruel's daughters away from a well of water, Moses stepped in to protect the women and to water their flocks. He did not stop and ponder the situation. He helped them because it was the right thing and the kind thing to do. He attended to their need when they needed it (Exodus 2:15-17).

Moses' spontaneity speaks volumes to us. How many times have we missed an opportunity for kindness because we procrastinated ("I'm too famished – I'll help my friend tomorrow")? Perhaps we felt as if everything had to be perfect before we could be kind ("My hair's a wreck – I can't face my new neighbors moving in"). Maybe we felt our efforts would not be good enough ("My last roast was literally a burnt offering!"). Even little acts of kindness can mean so much if the recipient needs it right then. Often we need to act quickly or the opportunity to meet that need will be lost. As Ralph Waldo Emerson stated, "You cannot do a kindness too soon, for you never know how soon it will be too late." [5]

• **Be kind when you have had time to think.** During the reign of Israel's king Jehoram, the city of Samaria was in dire straits. It was besieged by the Aramean army led by their king Ben-Hadad (2 Kings 7:3-20). People were starving, and mothers were killing their babies and eating them just to stay alive! Four lepers at the city gate decided to surrender to the Arameans. What did they have to lose?

When the lepers ventured over to the Arameans' camp, they found it abandoned! The Lord had caused the Arameans to hear the sound of chariots, horses and a great army that terrified the soldiers so badly that they ran for their lives. In the aftermath of the enemies' quick exit, the lepers were living it up – eating, drinking, taking plunder and hiding it to protect their bounty.

Then they had time to think about how it was not right to keep their good news to themselves. They decided to alert the starving people of Samaria. Because of their kindness, the city was saved from starvation. What would have happened if the lepers had not thought about the situation and done what they could to help?

In our lives there is a place for impulsive, spur-of-the-moment kindness. There is also room for planned, deliberate acts of kindness to brighten the days of others. Who knows – it might even change their lives! We may never know what effect our kindness might have on the life of someone else. As Vern McLellan quipped, "Be kind to everybody. You never know who might show up on the jury at your trial!" [6]

Especially in dealing with other women, it is so important to be kind – even if they are snippy, crude or unkind to us. We might not know everything they are going through. As Plato remarked, "Be kind, for everyone you meet is fighting a hard battle." [7] Our kindness might make all the difference. Don't leave home without it!

Searching Further

1. What country was sending marauding bands to Israel to force them into slavery? Into whose home was the little maid made a slave?

2. What was Naaman's status in the army of Aram? What was his medical problem?

3. How did the little girl show kindness to Naaman? Does this sort of kindness come naturally?

4. Why do you think Paul told Titus to teach older women to teach younger women to be kind? How do you think they taught them?

5. What are some ways even preschoolers can be unkind? What are some examples of children who chose to be kind?

6. How did Joseph show kindness to his brothers? How do you think they felt, especially when they had been so malicious to him?

7. What did the Good Samaritan have to do to take care of the half-dead man along the Jericho road?

8. How did Moses show on-the-spot kindness to Ruel's daughters?

9. How did the thoughtfulness of the lepers in the Aramean camp save the people of Samaria?

10. What are some ways we can show kindness every day?

Who Else?
Who else was a servant who shared good news (Acts 12:13-14)?

Safari Savvy

Choosing a Kinder Response

You see your neighbor coming. You know what usually happens when you two get together – you both bad-mouth your mutual friend. But now you are more conscious of the harm that this trash talk does to everyone involved. Now you want to respond differently. You want to change the negative dynamic to a positive one. You want to heal instead of tear people apart: "Reckless words pierce like a sword, but the tongue of the wise brings healing" (Proverbs 12:18). What better time than now to start to change the way you interact with your neighbor – even in a small way. Anticipate what you can say or do to make a difference. You could even rehearse your responses. The point is to try to respond in a kinder and healthier way.

You may try to change what you and your neighbor do together (for example, taking a walk instead of sitting with coffee). Invite another friend who does not know your friend and/or will not engage in the catty chat.

When the talk turns to your mutual friend, interject a positive comment. If you neighbor gets stuck in the hole of mudslinging, find a way to change the subject. Utilize Paul's list of "whatevers" in Philippians 4:8 as a guide for thinking and talking about uplifting things and ideas.

Make an effort to get to know better the one you have been talking about so you can better understand her. Try to develop compassion for her. Look for the positive in her so you will have something good to say about her.

Bring up the topic of relational aggression with your neighbor. Tell her about your new resolve. Ask her to join you! [8]

Chapter 5

Queen of
the Jungle

W e may have heard that the lion reigns as king of the jungle, but the truth is that lions do not even live in the jungle! Contrary to all the lions running through the Tarzan movies we have seen, the lion's principal habitat is the grassy plains known as the savanna. It is even iffy whether the lion holds the crown for "king of the beasts." A solitary lion can be backed down and killed by elephants, water buffalo and hyenas.[1]

In the world of women's relationships, the title of "Queen of the Jungle" is up for grabs too. You have probably met one of these royal bully types yourself. Everything has to be her way; and if it isn't her way, she expects you to change it – and right now!

Cheryl Dellasega, in her book *Mean Girls Grown Up*, names this type of woman the "queen bee."[2] Queen bees are women bullies who stake out their territorial authority and jealously protect it. This description is taken from nature, where queen bees in a hive reign over the worker bees and kill any rival queens. Similarly, it is in this destructive behavior that human queen bees excel – intimidation, manipulation, exclusion and exploitation. Queen bees are not a new phenomenon. There was one back in the Old Testament who was a bona fide queen!

The Princess and the P ... (Power)

A princess born in a morally corrupt gutter – that describes Athalia. As the daughter of Ahab, one of Israel's most evil kings, she was exposed to Baal worship with all its debauchery. Ahab probably had several wives (2 Kings 10:1), and Scripture does not tell us if Athalia was Jezebel's daughter. But most likely, the notorious pagan queen had some detrimental influence on Athalia.[3]

During Athalia's childhood, diplomacy between warring Israel and Judah was less strained. To facilitate better relations, Athalia's father, Ahab, arranged a marriage between Athalia and Jehoram, oldest son of Jehoshaphat, king of Judah (2 Kings 8:18).[4] In coming to Judah, Athalia brought her Baal worship with her. At the age of 32, Jehoram became king, and he shared Athalia's commitment to idolatry and paganism (2 Chronicles 21:4-6). His wife seemed to be a driving force in Jehoram's evil life: "He walked in the ways of the kings of Israel, as the house of Ahab had done, *for he married a daughter of Ahab.* He did evil in the eyes of the LORD" (2 Kings 8:18, author's emphasis).

After eight years of moral decay, Jehoram died in great pain from bowel disease, and Athalia was left a widow with one son, Ahaziah. At the youthful age of 22, Ahaziah ascended the throne with his mother playing a major part in his decision making, "For his mother encouraged him in doing wrong" (2 Chronicles 22:3). After only reigning a year, he was put to death by the men of his rival Jehu.

No one was powerful enough to take the reins of the kingdom in hand. It was in this vacuum of power that Athalia saw her chance. The stage was set for a bully to take over the kingdom of Judah, and Athalia filled the role. She set about to massacre the royal family, including her male grandchildren who were heirs to the throne. Confident then that no one would challenge her, she proclaimed herself queen of Judah.

A Woman Defies the Bully

Athalia's plan might have succeeded completely if it were not for the spunk, bravery and quick thinking of Ahaziah's sister, Jehosheba. As King Jehoram's daughter, this princess and wife of the priest Jehoiada was in a unique position to act. She defied the bully queen by saving

Joash, Ahaziah's infant son. She, along with her husband, Jehoiada, hid Joash in the temple while Athalia ruled the land for six years.

When Joash was 7, the priest Jehoiada led a counterrevolution to depose Queen Athalia and crown Joash as the new king. He obtained the allegiance of the commanders and leaders of Judah. After having these men guard the temple with King David's weapons, Jehoiada brought out Joash to crown him. The people ran and cheered, "Long live the king."

When Athalia heard the commotion, she ran to the temple and saw the king with all the people rejoicing and singing. She tore her robes and shouted, "Treason! Treason!" The soldiers seized her and took her outside the temple, where they killed her. Jehoiada placed Joash on the throne, and the people rejoiced because their bully queen was dead!

In the entire history of God's people, no other queen ever sat on David's throne. That Athalia was queen for six years speaks of the power she wielded over the bullied nation of Judah. Working within the providence of God and the help of others, a woman took steps to eventually stand up to the bully queen. Generations of God's people praise Him that Jehosheba was willing to take that risk!

Why Do Bullies Bully?

We see in Athalia a dramatic example of a bully who went to extremes to get what she wanted. She did whatever it took – even murdering her own grandsons! Why would any woman stoop to such immoral depths?

Athalia's character was no doubt forged in her tender years. When she was younger, Athalia might have even been a victim of bullying from another queen bee – Jezebel. In lashing back, she grew up to retaliate and "sting" anyone who got in her way. Or Athalia might have been a lifelong bully whose mode of survival was to respond aggressively every time she was threatened.[5]

Whatever Athalia's reason for bullying, it came down to the root cause of any bullying – lack of control.[6] Women bully to control others and feel important. They want to feel better about themselves, so they bully others to get attention, gain popularity, punish other women they are jealous of, or have "fun" at others' expense.[7]

Ironically, the life of a bully is often full of baffling paradoxes. The bully wants to appear superior to others, but deep down she feels inferior. She feels the need to boss others around to obtain power when inside she often feels powerless. To make herself feel important, she has to belittle others. She might look as if she has it all together when in truth she is falling apart.[8]

The saddest thing about a bully is that she longs for attention and respect, but the response she evokes from others is fear and hate. Women may cower in her presence, but they despise her behind her back and rejoice when she falls. This was graphically seen at Athalia's death and the crowning of King Joash, when "[A]ll the people of the land rejoiced. And the city was quiet, because Athalia had been slain with the sword at the palace" (2 Kings 11:20).

The Silent Epidemic

Unfortunately, women bullying women is becoming a silent epidemic that many women witness but do not do anything to stop. This is especially true in the workplace, where half of the bullies are women.[9] Women bully women more than any other gender combination. Women tend to bully via a network of other women. Studies have found that three-fourths of adult bullying involved more than one person with women as the ringleaders.[10]

Unlike childhood bullies who usually victimize the weak or unusual child, these adult "queens of mean" often target other women who are stronger, more efficient, more popular and more professional with good communication and social skills. Why do bullies pick on such women? Bullies view capable women as threats to their professional or social standing whether the bully has more or less authority than the target. Sometimes a worker will torment her boss, or a PTA member will bully the committee chairman.[11]

Bullying has taken a techno-turn for the worse with the age of the Internet. Cyber bullying occurs when victims are insulted via blogs, social networking websites and e-mails. An ugly anonymous instant message can inflict emotional wounds by poisonous words. E-mails can get heatedly vicious between women, and a quick keystroke can pass the exchange to an audience in seconds. Other virtual bullies hide behind the anonymity of a nickname and taunt and intimidate others. They find it easy to shoot other people down because they do not seem "real."

However, the harm they inflict on others is real.[12] The damage is so real that numerous health conditions may exist in targeted women that had not existed beforehand.[13] For all these reasons, we cannot just pretend bullying does not occur. Something needs to be done.

How to Respond

So how do you respond to bullying? What if you or a friend is singled out by a bully? Each situation is different, and we should pray for wisdom in dealing with anyone who persecutes us.

Try to look objectively at what is going on. Try to understand why the bullying is taking place. Is the victim threatening or intimidating to the bully? Or is it possible that the victim is acting in a way to invite bullying? If this is the case, she needs to act more assertively without being overly confident or excessively timid. Whenever we are unjustly criticized or harassed, we need to stand up for ourselves.[14]

In certain circumstances, it is just best to ignore the bully. Ignoring her takes away her power over people.[15] However, sometimes the bully cannot be ignored. Sometimes it helps to meet face-to-face with the bully to ask her to stop the harassment. Take a witness with you. Avoid any attempts to debate the bully, because you could get entangled in a losing verbal battle.[16]

It is a good idea to document all encounters, even those considered insignificant. Even trivial interactions, taken in total, might demonstrate a pattern and show that the bullying was more than an isolated event. Writing things down can also help us know if we are being reasonable in our perspective.[17]

Talk with someone, in authority if possible, who can help before the situation gets worse. We need to make it known that if the bullying continues, the bully's tactics may spread to others.

If your friend is being bullied, you could support her by preparing and signing a statement describing the bully's actions. You also could testify at a meeting regarding the bullying. Get others to admit that they have seen the bully's unacceptable behavior. Plan how the group can confront the bully to hold her accountable. Resist the bully's "divide and conquer" antics to turn the group against the target.[18]

If you have done everything you can and the bullying does not stop, you need to consider making a change. How about changing committees, enrolling in a different class, or taking a new job?

Jehosheba did not stand by and do nothing while Athalia murdered the heirs to the throne. She did what she could at the appropriate time and place. We can take a lesson from her actions.

The good news is that bullies can change. They can learn to treat other women with respect. God's love exemplified in our empathy, kindness and respect can change the coldest heart – if it is willing to change. It may take a while, but it is possible. Who knows – with time, maybe a bully will one day turn into a buddy!

Searching Further

1. Who was Athalia's father? What pagan queen was probably an influence on her? What kinds of evil influence might this queen have had on Athalia?

2. What might have prompted Ahab to arrange a marriage between Athalia and Jehoram? What did Athalia bring with her to the marriage?

3. How long did Jehoram's reign last? How did he die? Who became the new king? How did his mother influence him?

4. How did the new king die? Who became the new ruler? Why?

5. What did Athalia do to ensure no one would challenge her? What did Jehosheba and Jehoiada do? How did this couple challenge the queen at the right time? What happened to her?

6. What are some experiences from a woman's childhood that may make her more likely to choose to bully later when she is an adult?

7. What is the root cause of any bullying? What are some other reasons women might choose to be bullies?

8. What are some of the paradoxes in a bully's life? What are some differences in the victims of child bullies and adult bullies? Why?

9. In what ways has the Internet given bullies an expanded venue?

10. What are some things that we as Christian woman can do to deal with a bully? Why is it important to be "shrewd as snakes and innocent as doves" in our interactions with bullies (Matthew 10:16)?

Who Else?

Who else was a queen bully (1 Kings 21:1-16)?

How Can I Really Help?

Standing up for a girlfriend or co-worker who is being bullied is just one way to show support for the women in our lives during difficult times. When a friend is hurting, Solomon wisely perceived that it is just as important to know what *not* to do as it is to know what to do: "Like one who takes away a garment on a cold day, or like vinegar poured on soda, is one who sings songs to a heavy heart" (Proverbs 25:20).

• **Sick family member.** Your friend, as a caregiver, is often overlooked and is a candidate for depression, frustration and anger. Do not increase her anxiety by asking, "Have you found the best doctor?" Let her vent without judging her. Find specific ways to help instead of asking the old standby, "If there's anything you need, just let me know." Providing the daily necessities such as preparing a meal, baby-sitting the children, or offering to pick up groceries means a lot.

• **Job loss.** In losing a job, your friend has suffered a huge blow to her ego. Do not fuel her insecurity by asking, "Did you hear back from that employer?" or "How will you pay the bills?" You can follow her lead by listening and then gently encouraging her to move forward. Look for job leads you can pass on to her.

• **Death in the family.** Check to see what your grieving friend needs, whether coordinating food for funeral guests, helping with final decisions, or writing thank-you notes. Do not expect her grief to follow a set timetable. Allow her to grieve in her own way, and support her with your presence.

• **Serious illness.** Friends face illness in different ways. Do not disappear, but don't rush in with advice either. Listen for clues on what would help her the most. Sometimes sending an encouraging card, accompanying her for a doctor's appointment, or offering to take her out will do wonders.[19] "A friend loves at all times, and a brother is born for adversity" (Proverbs 17:17).

Chapter 6

Blabbermouth Birds

One summer morning as we slept in a Guatemalan village, we were awakened by the song of an unknown jungle bird. Its melody was so unique that we were mesmerized by the sound. After a while, however, the bird's repetitive rhapsody got on our nerves. We had just about had enough of the blabbermouth bird. You can understand why – it was about 4 a.m.!

The world is full of another kind of blabbermouth bird. These beings cannot seem to keep their mouths shut. The wise man referred to these birds in Ecclesiastes: "Do not revile the king even in your thoughts, or curse the rich in your bedroom, because a bird of the air may carry your words, and a bird on the wing may report what you say" (Ecclesiastes 10:20).

How many times have you wondered, "That was supposed to be a secret – how did she find that out?" It was from the babbling of the ubiquitous blabbermouth bird!

This babbling, otherwise known as gossip, might on the surface seem innocent, but it can be dangerous, even deadly. Because gossip intrigues us, we often miss its potential for evil, especially in damaging women's relationships. Dreams have been derailed, careers ruined and families torn apart because of gossip. In fact, Paul put gossipers in the company of some pretty bad characters – "filled with every kind of wickedness, evil, greed and depravity ... full of envy, murder, strife, deceit and malice. They are gossips" (Romans 1:29). He especially cautioned some young widows to avoid gossip at all costs.

What's a Widow to Do?

Widows who lived during the time of the Roman Empire found themselves in an extremely difficult predicament. Due to the ravages of war, disease and hard physical labor, men were lucky to live to old age. The average life expectancy was about 25 years (and some scholars consider that optimistic).[1] Subsequently, wives who outlived their husbands were left widows at a young age and found it hard to make an honest living. They were often driven to prostitution just to support themselves.[2]

To remedy the problem of caring for widows, the early church put together a list of widows who had no family. In 1 Timothy 5:9-10 Paul gave Timothy qualifications for the widows who could be enrolled in such a program. Women over 60 who had served the Lord faithfully were honored with compensation for the rest of their lives. It was understood that they would not marry but commit themselves to good works.

Paul instructed Timothy that younger widows should not be placed on this list (1 Timothy 5:11-15). He thought that, because of their age, it would be more difficult for them to keep their lifelong commitment to the church. Instead of being overcome by their sexual desires and abandoning their pledge to Christ, they were advised by Paul to marry again, raise children and manage their homes. He believed their lives would then be busy and productive.[3]

If this were not the case, the apostle explained how easy it would be for these women (and any woman for that matter) to become lazy when they didn't have much to do. They would end up restlessly gadding about from house to house, gossiping and meddling in other people's business as busybodies, "saying things they ought not to" (1 Timothy 5:13).

We can see why Paul considered gossip detrimental to personal relationships, especially when women are involved. So what is gossip, and what can we do about it?

"Shhhhhhh! It's a Secret!"

Whose ears do not perk up when they hear those words? The original meaning of "gossip" in Greek referred to the spreading of rumors or secrets, often to slander someone else. As a noun, it is synonymous with "talebearer," "tattler" and "whisperer." Even the Greek word itself – *psithyristes* – sounds like a whisper![4, 5]

Whether we whisper or not, we women love to talk! It is easy for our talk to degenerate quickly into gossip. Gossip is more than talking about someone; it involves talking against them.[6]

We speak of sharing "juicy gossip"; and like all tempting delicacies, we do not want to stop with just one![7] Proverbs 18:8 says it well: "The words of a gossip are like choice morsels; they go down to a man's inmost parts." When those juicy morsels are eaten with great relish and absorbed in our minds and hearts, we hunger for more![8]

The truth is that we bond with each other by sharing the details of our lives and the lives of others. We build on each other's points by adding "That happened to my mother too" or "My sister-in-law has that same problem with her husband." Through this sharing, women grow closer and can relate better to each other. Some women's friendships are even built on this sharing of confidences.[9] In fact, certain women delight in being the conduit through which secret but juicy tidbits of news pass on to others. Other women choose particular friends just to find out what they know.

Sharing secrets can make us closer friends, but it can also tear friends apart. "A perverse man stirs up dissension, and a gossip separates close friends" (Proverbs 16:28). We need to watch what we are sharing. What we say to one person in confidence might be repeated and misunderstood by another. As the wise man wrote, "A gossip betrays a confidence; so avoid a man who talks too much" (20:19). It is often wiser to keep confidences to ourselves. If we feel it necessary to share with a friend, be sure she can be trusted: "A gossip betrays a confidence, but a trustworthy man keeps a secret" (11:13). No wonder Benjamin Franklin quipped, "Three may keep a secret, if two of them are dead."[10]

When the Truth Hurts

Gossip is not only speaking untruths. It also includes speaking the truth that might hurt someone else. Speaking the truth does not make it acceptable to say hurtful things about others. As author Frank A.

Clark stated, "Gossip needn't be false to be evil – there's a lot of truth that shouldn't be passed around."[11]

However, there are times when the truth must be told if it protects someone. Although it might be unflattering or even defamatory to someone else, it might be important to let others know. For instance, it is appropriate to tell the truth about a scam artist, embezzler or sex offender. We should pray for wisdom to handle each situation wisely.

More often, however, we are in gossip situations in which we have a choice to talk or listen or even leave. We can ask ourselves three important questions when we wonder if we should share something or listen:

(1) **Is it true?** Are you sure the news you just heard is true? Have you ever heard something like: "We really need to pray for Holly. Jenny told her sister that Mark thought that Sandy saw Holly …" If you doubt the origin of the information, check the source. As the writer Sir Alan Herbert observed, "If nobody ever said anything unless he knew what he was talking about, a ghastly hush would descend upon the earth."[12]

(2) **Is it kind?** Appearances can be deceiving. We can misunderstand what we see or hear and repeat something unkind that could hurt something deeply. One Christian lady reported to another lady in their congregation that a single teenager was pregnant. Later the lady discovered that the girl was wearing a big top that only made her look that way! "When words are many, sin is not absent, but he who holds his tongue is wise" (Proverbs 10:19).

(3) **Is it necessary?** Do we really need to tell everything we know or say everything we think? What is our motive? Why do we feel that we have to share a certain bit of information? If there is not a good reason, we need to let the information end with us. An anonymous sage had it right: "There is nothing wrong with having nothing to say – unless you insist on saying it."[13]

The Deadly Forms of Gossip

Beware of these particular forms of gossip that are especially dangerous for us as Christian women. They look so harmless on the surface, but we can easily get caught in our mouth-traps! That is what makes it so easy for us to become willing participants and taken in by their evil.

• **I'll-tell-you-anyway gossip.** This form of gossip can wind its way through the "godly grapevine." Thinly disguised as compassion and concern, it can wound just as deeply as malicious tale bearing. You can identify it by comments such as: "Don't tell anyone, but I think you ought to know because you might want to put this on your prayer list" or "It's wrong, and I can't believe she would say that about the elder's wife." We need to differentiate between genuine concern and general nosiness! The trouble with gossip is that, as Vern McLellan puts it, it "always seems to travel fastest over grapevines that are slightly sour."[14]

• **I'm-just-listening gossip.** Although we may try to keep from talking too much or saying anything at all, we still might fall in this category. If we participate by listening, we are encouraging the gossiper and fueling her on. We need to have the courage to say, "I have to go," or "I can't listen anymore." "A wicked man listens to evil lips; a liar pays attention to a malicious tongue" (Proverbs 17:4). Perhaps if we were not such avid listeners, gossipers would not be such avid talkers!

• **I-don't-know-them gossip.** Often women talk about people and organizations that they might not know personally. They think, "What's the harm? I don't know them (and they might not know me)." Our questions should really be, "Am I honoring God by taking part in this? Am I tearing people down even if I don't know them?"[15] We need to try to build up instead of tear down. Paul wrote, "Do not let any unwholesome talk come out of your mouths, but only what is helpful for building others up according to their needs, that it may benefit those who listen" (Ephesians 4:29).

Keeping It Interesting

Some women may wonder what they will talk about if they cannot gossip! We do not have to gossip to be an interesting conversationalist. We can take some cues from Jesus as we look for some alternatives to gossip.

• **Share your sense of humor.** Although Jesus could be serious, He also liked to have a good time. Because Jesus liked people, He was invited to their homes and enjoyed their company as He ate and drank with them (Matthew 11:19). His interaction with people included wry humor that we often miss in our contemporary culture. Such ludicrous hyperboles as an eye with a plank of wood trying to see another's speck of sawdust (7:3-5), a camel passing through the eye of a needle (19:24), or one straining a gnat while he swallows a camel (23:24), no doubt brought smiles to His listeners' faces.[16]

Isn't it fun to be around women who can see the funny side of life and who have an uncanny ability to laugh at themselves? We have five senses, but they are not complete without the sixth – a healthy sense of humor! We should try to exercise our "funny bone" more, especially when circumstances can easily suck all the joy out of us. Just looking for the laughter in our everyday lives lightens our own load and the loads of others. As humorist Josh Billings remarked, "Laughing is the sensation of feeling good all over and showing it principally in one spot."[17]

• **Ask perceptive questions.** Jesus was not an ostrich-with-His-head-in-the-sand kind of guy. He was interested in others. He focused on the people He met because each person was important to Him. One way He showed He cared was by the perceptive questions He asked (John 5:6; 6:5, 66-67; 8:10). We too need to go beyond the perfunctory "How are you?" and ask others what is going on in their lives. This does not mean nosey questions but rather thoughtful ones. The more we listen to others' answers, the more we will discover about them and the better we can understand them.

• **Learn to tell a good story.** Jesus was a marvelous storyteller. His parables delighted and amazed the crowds who followed Him. His stories were often a clever way of teaching God's truths in a way His listeners would remember. Why can't we cultivate the art of telling a good story today? Don't you enjoy listening to another woman who has stories to tell about fascinating people, places and things? If we developed this art, it would guarantee that people would find us more interesting!

• **Tell the good news.** Wherever Jesus went, He shared the good news of the kingdom. Throughout the villages of Palestine, He spoke "gracious words" and gave hope to people again (Luke 4:18-22). What better way to use our tongues than to share the best news anyone could hear – the gospel! Just like Paul, we need to pray for boldness, grace and wisdom: "Be wise in the way you act toward outsiders; make the most of every opportunity. Let your conversation be always full of grace, seasoned with salt, so that you may know how to answer everyone" (Colossians 4:5-6). If we were busier sharing the good news, we would not have time to gossip!

Searching Further

1. With what other sins did Paul classify gossip (Romans 1:29)?

2. What was the average life span of a man during the time of the Roman Empire? Why did he die so young? What was the plight of his widow in this situation?

3. What commitment did some Christian widows make when their husbands died? Why did Paul later condemn them?

4. What did Paul tell younger widows to avoid? What did he advise them to do instead (1 Timothy 5:13-14)?

5. How do women usually bond? Why does that make it even more important to avoid gossip?

6. What are some circumstances when we might want to share information that might show others in a bad light?

7. What are three questions to help us determine what information to share with others?

8. What are particular forms of gossip that are especially dangerous for Christian women?

9. What were some occasions in which Jesus was serious? When did He show that He enjoyed life?

10. What are some alternatives to gossip in our daily conversations?

Who Else?

Who else were busybodies (2 Thessalonians 3:11)?

Celebrating Good News

What is one of the first things you want to do when you hear good news? Share it with a good friend! Solomon wrote, "A cheerful look brings joy to the heart, and good news gives health to the bones" (Proverbs 15:30). Good news gives us cause to celebrate, and good friends can find a myriad of ways to celebrate!

• **Birthdays.** Whether we look at birthdays as good news or bad depends on our outlook! How better to commemorate what we have learned from the last year than with our friends. One mother made her daughter's 21st birthday very special by asking her (the mother's) friends to write down any wisdom or inspiration they had gathered from their 40-plus years of accumulated life experience.

• **Marriage.** Hold a teacup party and ask each guest to bring a wrapped teacup (with a prayer or advice, if desired) that reflects the giver's personality. The bride-to-be opens the teacups and uses them for a tea party. Afterward she is reminded of each friend when she uses the cups.

• **Babies.** Put together a time capsule with items that personify the era of the child's birth.[18] Borrowing from African village tradition, speculate on why the child is born at this time and place by answering the question "What are we needing now that this child is sent to add among us?"[19] You could add a spiritual dimension to these observations as Mordecai did with Esther's timely rise to become queen in God's people's history (Esther 4:14).

One

Target
Practice

I f we were to plan on taking a safari to the jungle to hunt wild
game, we would first need to practice hitting a target. Admittedly,
some of us could not hit the side of a barn, much less a bull's-eye!
Whether we aim a gun or a camera, we would need to take some practice shots first. Target practice would be a necessity!

Another kind of huntress roams our landscape and uses other people as emotional target practice. She aims intentionally and hits her
mark wherever she can. First Samuel gives us a look at one of these
huntresses.

Married for Children

Hannah was her target, and Peninnah took aim often (1 Samuel 1).
Her verbal missiles usually hit Hannah where it hurt the most, in her
most vulnerable area – Hannah's childlessness. With several children
running about her, Peninnah was Hannah's rival. These two wives of
Elkanah found what women in polygamous marriages throughout history have found – polygamy invariably pits the wives against each other. It was not an accident that God intended one man and one woman
in marriage.

Although Elkanah loved Hannah best, it is possible that he married
Peninnah to provide offspring when his favorite wife, Hannah, could

not provide them. In those days, when a woman could not have children, her position in the household was tenuous. She could be ostracized, discarded or demoted in status within the family. People viewed childbearing as a sign of God's richest blessing, whereas barrenness was often seen as God's punishment.[1]

The culture at that period of time supported that belief. In Bible times it was important for a family to have children and lots of them. Children were needed to work the fields and tend the herds. They cared for their parents when they got old and carried on their memory when they died. Sometimes they increased the wealth and prestige of the household through contracts of marriage.[2]

Set Up for Rivalry

It probably was not intentional, but Elkanah set up his wives for rivalry from the start. Peninnah bore Elkanah the children he desired, but Hannah possessed his heart. Scripture calls Peninnah a "rival," and both women felt the pressure of a competition. Peninnah "kept provoking her [Hannah] in order to irritate her" (1 Samuel 1:6). This provoking was not an occasional jab. It went on "year after year" (v. 7).

Every year at a special day of worship and sacrifice, Hannah's childlessness would be rubbed in her face like salt poured into a fresh wound. Peninnah and her children were given portions of the sacrificial meat. Because he loved Hannah, Elkanah tried to compensate by giving Hannah a double portion. Peninnah's cruel words about Hannah's childlessness would upset Hannah so much that she could not enjoy what was at that time a special treat. In fact, Peninnah's spitefulness drove Hannah to tears.

Elkanah did not help the situation when he asked Hannah, "Hannah, why are you weeping? Why don't you eat? Why are you downhearted? Don't I mean more to you than ten sons?" (1 Samuel 1:8). His love for Hannah did not take the place of her longing for children and all they meant to a woman of those times.

Power for the Powerless

Hannah could have felt powerless in such a situation beyond her control. The two people closest to her did not help her. Her husband did not truly understand, and the other wife vexed her to tears. Hannah might have resigned herself to a hopeless future.

But Hannah knew where her real strength and power lay – in the Lord Almighty! She knew that the house of God in Shiloh housed the ark of the covenant, which symbolized the presence of God. She poured out her heart and vowed that if God would give her a son, she would give him back. Eli the priest thought that her silent but moving lips were the result of drunkenness. But she explained that she was praying out of anguish and grief. With Eli's blessing, she left with renewed hope and promise.

In due time, she had a son she named Samuel. When he was weaned at about 2 or 3 years of age, she and Elkanah presented him to Eli for him to be Eli's helper. It must have been a difficult parting, but God blessed the couple with more children – three more sons and two daughters (1 Samuel 2:21). Hannah's prayer of praise to God included the statement that "She who was barren has borne seven children, but she who has had many sons pines away" (v. 5). We do not know if this refers symbolically to the two rival wives, but we do know Peninnah was never mentioned in Scripture again!

Deflecting the Attack

When another woman is mean and spiteful to us like Peninnah was to Hannah, we might believe that we can do nothing and that our situation is hopeless. It would be good to look to Hannah as our example.

First, she prayed about the matter. She had confidence in the Lord's power. God is our greatest source of power for change, and we can tap that power through prayer. If we turn our troubles over to Him, He can give us insights and wisdom to change what we can and peace to deal with what we cannot change. "Do not be anxious about anything, but in everything, by prayer and petition, with thanksgiving, present your requests to God. And the peace of God, which transcends all understanding, will guard your hearts and your minds in Christ Jesus" (Philippians 4:6-7). God cares when we are mistreated. "Cast all your anxiety on him because he cares for you" (1 Peter 5:7).

Next, Hannah talked to someone she could trust who could help – Eli. It was good for her to talk to someone objective who could understand.

Eli gave her the assurance she needed. We are often afraid to share our problems with others because we do not trust them. Perhaps we are hesitant to "spill the beans" to someone for fear that she will invite everyone she knows for bean soup! What a comfort it is to find someone who will share our burden without repeating our situation to others!

Sometimes we are afraid to share with others because we might look inadequate. None of us are perfect, and it is okay not to be perfect. In fact, others can more likely empathize with us if they know that we have flaws. We will experience a great sense of relief if we can share our burden with someone who cares. "Carry each other's burdens, and in this way you will fulfill the law of Christ" (Galatians 6:2).

Lastly, Hannah did not retaliate. She could have taunted Peninnah about how much Elkanah loved her as "Wife Number One," but she did not. Hannah knew that God would avenge spiteful words and cruelty in His own time. Paul's words speak to us today: "Bless those who persecute you; bless and do not curse. ... Do not repay anyone evil for evil. Be careful to do what is right in the eyes of everybody. If it is possible, as far as it depends on you, live at peace with everyone. Do not take revenge, my friends, but leave room for God's wrath, for it is written: 'It is mine to avenge; I will repay,' says the Lord. On the contrary: 'If your enemy is hungry, feed him; if he is thirsty, give him something to drink. In doing this, you will heap burning coals on his head.' Do not be overcome by evil, but overcome evil with good" (Romans 12:14, 17-21). The only way to stop the "cycle of mean" is by using kindness instead of cruelty.

The Mommy Wars

Today many mothers find themselves right in the middle of a cycle of mean. It is a combat zone of the "Mommy Wars," where mothers use one another for target practice. Mother-to-mother conflict can begin early – even before pregnancy. Verbal volleys bounce back and forth in a "Battle of the Babies." Who is the first in a group of women to get pregnant? After the baby is born, who is the first to teethe, walk and talk? Who goes to the best preschool? Who starts playing a musical instrument or participates in a sport? Then how many instruments or sports do they play? The "one-upwomanship" comparisons keep on going. "I can beat that. Wait 'til you hear what *my* kid did. ..."

For some, the competition-by-virtue-of-children never seems to end. From preschool to college to marriage to career, mothers tout the achievements of their offspring. "He got straight A's and won scholarships to 15 colleges." "She got her size 4 gown on sale – for only $2,500!" "He works for a Fortune 500 company and hopes to be CEO someday."[3]

What makes a mother feel she must compete through her children? Often her insecurities drive her to try to live her life through her offspring. She sees her children as an extension of herself. Perhaps her life was not as successful as she wished, and she wants more for her children. No matter the endeavor, her vanity comes into play – whenever the child looks good, the mother looks good too!

Make Them All Look Good

Whether we have children or not, we need to use discretion and be sensitive to the feelings of others. A mother droning on and on about her child's many accomplishments can grow very tiresome. If we have children, we need to be honest and ask ourselves, "Am I acting like that?" Proverbs 27:2 points out: "Let another praise you, and not your own mouth; someone else, and not your own lips." The idea is not to brag about yourself (or your family) but let others do the praising. Sharing news about our children is one thing. Boasting about how great they are is another.

How much better it would be if we could affirm other children as well as our own – making them all look good! Getting involved in the lives of other children makes us less likely to be focused exclusively on our own. This involvement might include becoming a part of group efforts such as sports teams or scout troops or perhaps teaching a class. Or it might mean taking an individual interest in other children, such as being kind to our daughter's best friend. In lifting other children up instead of dragging them down, we can model and teach our children a generous spirit instead of a mean, competitive one.

The Games Mommies Play

We also need to lift other women up. Women need each other, especially in the "passages" of life. We can provide crucial support as our children grow from teethers to teens. During the thorny periods of our child's development, how beneficial it is to have another mother with whom to commiserate! In years past, mothers could share child-rearing tips as they chatted over the fence while hanging the laundry up to dry. Now we are more likely to compare notes in a children's play group, church mothers class or Internet parents interest group. Sometimes it just means sharing heart-to-heart with another mother in the grocery store or at the park.

Although some mothers take advantage of these opportunities, others seem to want to put on a facade of the "perfect family." Instead of sharing, mothers often hide or bury their problems. The sad result of all this is the lack of support during the crucial time of childbearing and child rearing. They miss helpful insights from other mothers. What a rich resource they deny themselves – each other!

Not only do some mothers neglect to share with each other, but they also use other children as pawns in their own toxic adult relationship games. "Don't let your daughter invite the new girl over," one mother might say to another. "Her mother snubbed me at the grocery store." Or one mom might whisper to another, "They say her mom is a flirt. We don't need her daughter near our boys, do we?"[4]

Excluding daughters from parties and clubs, spreading rumors, be-friending some and not others – these behaviors inflict double damage to child and mother. The girls wonder what they did wrong. What mother does not feel the pain when her daughter suffers from any of these indignities?[5]

Some mothers who might not stand up for themselves when they are mistreated are very protective of their children. Some, in fact, go to the extreme. The "mother bear" instinct kicks in, words get heated, and sometimes fists fly! If you have ever seen two mothers engaged in verbal or physical conflict over their children, you know that there is little fury more volatile than that of mothers!

Confrontation between mothers – or any women for that matter – is a definite part of women interacting with each other. The next chapter looks at ways to handle this conflict, which is an inevitable part of a woman's relationship jungle.

Searching Further

1. Why did Peninnah taunt Hannah? How did Hannah react to her persistent ridicule?

2. In Bible times, what were some cultural disadvantages of a barren wife? Why was it important for families to have children then?

3. Which wife did Elkanah love most? How did he try to show his love every year? What did Peninnah's cruelty cause Hannah to do on that special occasion?

4. Where did Hannah find solace? To whom did she explain her situation? What did he do? How did the Lord bless Hannah? How many more children did Hannah and Elkanah have?

5. How can we tap into the power of God (Philippians 4:6-7)?

6. Why are we sometimes afraid to share our problems with others?

7. Could Hannah have had a reason to deride Peninnah? Did Hannah retaliate? Why should we refuse to pay back evil for evil (Romans 12:14, 17-21)?

8. How are some ways mothers compete in the "Mommy Wars"? What are some ways we can affirm other children?

9. Why do women need each other in life's rites of passage?

10. How do some mothers use other children as pawns in their own toxic relationships?

Who Else?

Who else was barren who later had a son (Genesis 16:1; 25:21; 29:31; Judges 13:2; Luke 1:7)?

Broccoli in Our Teeth

Although we do not like to be targets for criticism, sometimes we need to hear it. After all, only a real friend will tell us if we have broccoli in our teeth! How often has a friend's frank advice saved us from embarrassment and helped us know what to do? "Faithful are the wounds of a friend; profuse are the kisses of an enemy" (Proverbs 27:6 ESV). A friend's honest feedback can help us see things we are too blind to see. Negative feedback is especially effective in helping us know where we need to improve and how we can change for the better.

You would think that women would help each other in this way more often than we do. But friends are often hesitant to share negative feedback because they do not want to hurt our feelings. It takes a true friend to say what needs to be said. It also takes a woman of real character to accept unflattering or critical comments without animosity. Neither task is easy.

Why not think of feedback as a gift instead of a gripe? Even better, why not *ask* for feedback? Perhaps friends would be more willing to share, and we would all gain from the process of giving and receiving this gift.

When we take the initiative and ask for feedback, it might help to ask ourselves some questions: Am I asking someone who has the expertise or insight I need? Am I specific about the kind of feedback I need? Do I understand her point? Am I being too proud or too sensitive to listen? Do I want to make the changes she suggested, or do I need to filter her comments?[6] Author Ruth Graham wrote, "Just pray for a tough hide and a tender heart."[7] Now that is advice worth taking!

Chapter 8

Hiding Behind the Ferns

I magine that on your trek through the jungle you spy a tiger who has not caught sight of you or your scent. He is hungry for his next meal and has not yet found the first course. While he is sizing up the terrain, you are sizing up your options. He can outrun and maybe even outwit you. How do you avoid this conflict? You hope for the best and hide behind the nearest ferns!

Some people approach all conflict this way – they hide behind the nearest ferns. They believe conflict is always wrong so they avoid it at all costs. It is true that anger, fighting and dissension are condemned in the Bible, but conflict by itself does not have to include these things. In fact, conflict can be healthy, even productive, if its outcome brings healing or progress. The key is how the conflict is handled.

Often problems arise when conflicts are not resolved. This leads to fighting, backbiting, gossip, arguing and discord. It can begin with a conflict between two people that mushrooms into something more. Philippians tells us about two such women who just could not agree.

Conflict's Ripple Effect

Euodia and Syntyche were two Christian ladies with uncommon names (to us) who had a very common problem – they could not agree. In fact, their disagreement was so widely known that Paul knew about it in far-off Rome, where he was imprisoned. He wrote a letter to the Christians in Philippi to encourage them, but nestled toward the end of the letter was a special plea to Euodia and Syntyche (Philippians 4:2-3). In essence he begged these women who had worked side by side with him in the cause of the gospel to hang up their boxing gloves and agree in the Lord. Their disagreement must have been over matters of opinion. Paul would not put up with doctrinal error, and he would have pointed out their problem (Galatians 1:8). Euodia and Syntyche's differences could have been due to a clash of personalities or just different perspectives.[1]

We do not know whether Euodia and Syntyche ever worked out their differences, but we do know it affected the believers and their unity. Imagine the two women's surprise when they were singled out in Paul's letter to the Philippians! They probably hung their heads in embarrassment and shame as their names were read before the church. They probably never thought their disagreement could have such a ripple effect – on them, on the church, even on Paul many miles away.

The same is true with our conflicts. We might never know the ripple effect they can have in splintering others' relationships as well as our own. No wonder Paul reminds us repeatedly that we have been called to live in peace and unity (2 Corinthians 13:11; Colossians 3:15). We are to "make every effort" to keep peace (Romans 14:19; Hebrews 12:14-15).

Paul's admonition to Euodia and Syntyche shows us that even the most dedicated, hardworking Christian women can disagree. Sooner or later, we will be involved in conflict. So how are we going to deal with it?

Approaching Conflict

We can approach conflict in a number of ways, and different situations call for different approaches. The first two are extremes that people often use without thinking.

• **Peekaboo Approach**. Every mother has hidden her face from a baby and then poked up her head to say "peekaboo!" When the baby does not see you, to him you do not exist. It is the same way in the "peekaboo" approach to conflict. If someone denies there is conflict and refuses to see it, to her it does not exist. Denial of the problem, however, does not make it go away. Just like a painful boil, it just festers, grows and eventually bursts.

An example of this approach is King David, who refused to take any disciplinary action against his son Amnon when he raped his sister Tamar. David was furious, but we do not read of him doing anything to discipline Amnon (2 Samuel 13:21). It was as if David denied that it had even happened. Finally the "boil burst," and Absalom took matters into his own hands by ordering his men to kill his guilty brother.

• **Stampeding Elephant Approach.** In this approach to conflict, you disagree with someone and the next minute you wonder what happened as you find yourself trampled and peeling yourself off the floor! The purpose of the stampeding elephant approach is to mow down the opponent, totally wiping her out with no consideration for her beliefs and feelings. The perpetrator is not interested in listening to what the problem really is. Instead she chooses a quick, if ineffective, solution just for the sake of a solution.

This was Simeon and Levi's solution when Prince Shechem raped their sister, Dinah. They deceitfully asked that every male in Shechem be circumcised. Then the brothers caught the Shechemites off guard by killing every male in the city, looting the plunder and carrying off the women and children who were left (Genesis 34).

• **Head-On Approach.** This approach is an alternative to the previous all-or-nothing approaches. It is tough to face a problem or disagreement head on, but it is often the best way to deal with it. It is better to see and understand whom you are dealing with and why. When feelings and beliefs are aired, there is a much better chance to work out our problems. Nehemiah was a master at this approach. He spurred the Jews on to repair the walls of Jerusalem despite the opposition from Sanballat and Tobiah (Nehemiah 4). His head-on approach finally resulted in the completion and dedication of the walls of Jerusalem.

The Styles of Conflict

When we are facing a conflict, we can deal with it in various ways. In their book *In the Company of Women*, Pat Heim, Susan A. Murphy and Susan K. Golant described how each of us have a predominant conflict style that we favor based on our personal predispositions, social skills and temperament.[2] They have elaborated on five basic conflict styles.[3] Although each style has its advantages and limitations, we can learn to use the best style for each situation we encounter. For example, a woman may use a different style with her supervisor to discuss an unfair office policy than she would with a longtime friend whose dog dug up her prized petunias. As you note the various styles, think about how you could use them to get along with other women.[4]

• **The Avoider.** Motto: "Leave well enough alone." Avoiding a conflict can mean that you stall, overlook or pass the buck instead of trying to address an issue. It can also mean dropping out and hiding.[5]

Jonah is a classic example of an avoider (Jonah 1–4). He did not want to face the Ninevites, Israel's enemy, much less preach to them. So he headed off in a ship to Tarshish, as far as he could go in the opposite direction. Like other avoiders, he could not escape forever. He eventually did what God asked.

In some situations, however, avoiding conflict can be beneficial. It might be wise to overlook a conflict if the issue is not important. You might waste time addressing an issue that you are powerless to change. Sometimes you need to back off to give yourself or others time to cool their tempers. Other times you just do not have enough facts or time to make an informed decision, so it would be best to wait or avoid the conflict altogether.[6]

• **The Collaborator.** Motto: "Two heads are better than one." Collaborating works to the advantage of both sides of a conflict. Each side may brainstorm to find creative alternatives. Collaborating can be useful when it is important to combine ideas from people of various backgrounds and views or when conflicting interests cannot be ignored or conceded. It is also crucial to collaborate when your purpose is to build relationships and dissolve animosities through understanding others' perspectives.[7]

Collaborating was used effectively when the apostles dealt with the widows of the Grecian Jews and the Hebraic Jews (Acts 6:1-7). The apostles gathered all the Christians together and asked the brethren to select seven men to minister to the widows. The apostles gave their blessing on the decision. Instead of ruling with an iron fist, the apostles gave the Grecian Jews responsibility in choosing the men and implementing the plan. They had a voice in solving the dilemma and owning the solution.

However, we can also see how impractical this style would be for some situations. For instance, if everyone in a family, group or organization had to be consulted every time a conflict arose, resolution would be cumbersome and time-consuming.[8]

• **The Accommodator.** Motto: "Kill your enemies with kindness." Accommodating, in this context, is putting the needs and desires of someone you disagree with above your own. It takes humility to yield to someone else's viewpoint or advantage when you could do otherwise. Accommodating is helpful when the outcome matters more to the other person than it does to you. It is also useful when it is more important to preserve harmony.[9]

Such was the case between Abram and Lot. Abram was an accommodator when he bowed to the preference of Lot in the choice of land of Canaan (Genesis 13). Abram's and Lot's herdsmen had been quarreling, and Abram suggested they all part company, giving Lot first choice. Lot selfishly chose the well-watered plain near Sodom, and Abram was left the land of Canaan.

Accommodating can have a downside. Often we as Christian women default to accommodating in conflict because we have been taught to get along and be nice. We can get to the point, however, where we are constantly helping others to achieve their goals at the expense of our own. There is a real chance that we can become resentful martyrs. It is important to aim for balance between accommodating and maintaining our self-respect.[10]

• **The Compromiser.** Motto: "Split the difference." Compromising is a form of sharing – "I'll give you something if you'll give me something." Your side will not get everything you want, but each side is willing to give up something so the matter can be resolved. Neither side dominates nor retreats, but both sides exchange concessions. When disagreeing will not get you any further, you compromise and then move on. Compromising can help build trust and open lines of communication. However, you do need to know the limits of how much you are willing to give up. You can feel cheated if you believe someone has taken undue advantage of you.[11]

David and Abner were compromisers. As a young warrior, David had originally served under Abner, commander of King Saul's army and Saul's cousin as well. When David rose to power after Saul's death, Abner supported Saul's son Ish-Bosheth as king of Israel. Then Ish-Bosheth accused Abner of sleeping with Saul's concubine Rizpah. Besides the moral implication, this accusation essentially meant Abner was usurping Ish-Bosheth's authority. Abner became so angry at this accusation that he defected to David's side. Abandoning his support of Ish-Bosheth, Abner agreed to bring all of Israel over to David to show that he would indeed be loyal to him. In exchange for David's extending his amnesty to Abner, David required that Abner return Michal, Saul's daughter and David's wife. With these things accomplished, David and Abner sealed their agreement with a feast to celebrate the deal (2 Samuel 3:6-21).[12]

• **The Competitor**. Motto: "Might makes right." Competing can mean you stand up for yourself, defend a position you feel is right, or just try to win or get your own way. It might include pulling rank or using force. It is more of a win-lose situation with no negotiation. Competing is helpful when quick decisive action is called for or unpopular actions must be taken. For example, sometimes there is one job opening, and two friends who really want the job must compete.[13]

David was a competitor. When Goliath brazenly defied God and the armies that served Him, David took on the giant – with a sling and five stones. David had God on his side, and he was victorious. That contest was the beginning of many battles that David fought against the enemies of the Lord (1 Samuel 17).

However, competition can have a downside. At its worst, it can lead to envy, jealousy, backbiting and fighting. The next chapter considers some problems that unhealthy competition poses for Christian women and their relationships.

Searching Further

1. Is conflict always bad? What are some of the problems that are caused when conflicts are not resolved?

2. What was Euodia and Syntyche's problem? How did Paul address it? Why was their problem most likely not doctrinal?

3. What ripple effect did the two women's problem have on the church? How do our conflicts have ripple effects?

4. What are two extreme approaches to conflict that people often use without thinking? What are some biblical examples of these approaches (Genesis 34; 2 Samuel 13:21)? What is an alternative to these approaches? What is a biblical example of this approach (Nehemiah 4)?

5. How did Paul deal with doctrinal conflict involving Peter (Galatians 2:11-14)? How did Peter later describe Paul (2 Peter 3:15)? How did Paul deal with conflict over a matter of opinion with Barnabas concerning Mark (Acts 15:36-41)? How did Paul later describe Mark (2 Timothy 4:11; 1 Peter 5:13)?

6. What is the motto for the Avoider conflict style? What are some advantages? What are some disadvantages? Who is an example of an avoider in the Bible?

7. What is the motto for the Collaborator conflict style? What are some advantages? What are some disadvantages? Who are examples of collaborators in the Bible?

8. What is the motto for the Accommodator conflict style? What are some advantages? What are some disadvantages? Who are examples of accommodators in the Bible?

9. What is the motto for the Compromiser conflict style? What are some advantages? What are some disadvantages? Who are examples of compromisers in the Bible?

10. What is the motto for the Competitor conflict style? What are some advantages? What are some disadvantages? Who is an example of a competitor in the Bible?

Who Else?

Who else caused conflict among God's people (Genesis 26:34-35)?

Repairing Your Friendships

Ralph Waldo Emerson knew what he was talking about when he observed, "Keep your friendships in repair."[14] Friends just do not always agree. Conflict can creep into the best of friendships. What can you do to preserve your relationship when the two of you do not see eye to eye?

If you and your friend are going to meet and talk, take several deep breaths right before your meeting. Calm down if you are angry. Talking to a mirror might help you see how your body language comes across to her. Is your jaw tight or fist clenched and you do not realize it? Try to relax!

You might approach her like this: "I see this from a different perspective. Can we talk about it?" Indecisive mumbling gives the impression that you are unsure of what you are saying, so speak loudly enough to be heard. However, do not raise your voice. "A gentle answer turns away wrath, but a harsh word stirs up anger" (Proverbs 15:1).

Talk about one thing at a time. It is usually easier to deal with one problem at a time instead of a myriad of issues. Let the other person finish what she is saying without interrupting her. Actively listen and then paraphrase what she has said to make sure you have really heard her. Try to understand her viewpoint. If you were in her shoes, you might feel the same way she does.[15, 16]

Pray that God will give you the wisdom to say the right thing and to keep your mouth shut when necessary. As author Ann Hibbard wrote, "An attitude of humility and love is the sweet, refreshing water that helps our friend swallow the bitter pill of confrontation. Without this, she will surely choke on it."[17]

Chapter 9

Getting Ahead, Falling Behind

Any real jungle adventurer eager to reach her destination knows the danger of getting too far ahead of her guide. In fact, it can spell disaster. You could make one false step and unknowingly land in a tiger pit or a net booby trap. You could fall off a precipice into a ravine if you stray off the trail. Or you could quickly lose your sense of direction and get lost in the undergrowth of the jungle.

Competition between women is a lot like hurrying to get ahead and then falling way behind, realizing that you are lost. What was so important to you seems, in perspective, not to be so important after all. It seems to be a futile race that no one really wins. We see that dramatically in the competition between Rachel and Leah.

On Your Mark, Get Set, Go!

We do not know when it started, but the competition between Rachel and Leah seemed to plague them for much of their adult lives. Their "one-upwomanship" went on for years; first one woman had the upper hand and then the other. The sisters were rivals in three arenas:

• **Beauty.** When these daughters of Laban are first described in the Bible, they are differentiated by their looks. Leah had "weak eyes," which is an ambiguous term in Hebrew (Genesis 29:17). It could have meant that Leah's eyes were weak in vision or in color or that they were not appealing or bright.[1,2] It also could have meant her eyes made her vulnerable, fragile and tender. These qualities were positive and might have given her a delicate quality.[3] Whatever Leah's qualities were, there was no question about Rachel's. She was "lovely in form, and beautiful" (Genesis 29:17). Leah paled in comparison to Rachel's head-to-toe good looks, and Jacob fell in love with Rachel.

• **Boys.** We can only guess how many of the local boys had their eyes on Rachel, but it was actually her cousin Jacob who won her heart. In fact, he worked seven years to pay Laban the *mohar*, or bride's price, because he had no money of his own.[4]

Finally on the wedding night, Laban substituted his older daughter, Leah, whom Jacob discovered to his chagrin the next morning. After the wedding week with Leah, Laban gave Rachel to Jacob, but he had to commit to work for Laban another seven years. What a way to start a marriage! Imagine Jacob waking up to Leah in the morning, exclaiming, "You're the wrong one!" No doubt both wives felt cheated that they must share their husband.

This unhappy situation set up both these women to suffer lives of resentment, jealousy and envy. Their struggle was vividly illustrated when Rachel wanted Leah's mandrakes, a plant thought in the East to be an aphrodisiac.[5] To Rachel's request, Leah replied, "Wasn't it enough that you took away my husband? Will you take my son's mandrakes too?" (Genesis 30:15). Jacob loved Rachel more than Leah, and Leah probably felt the pangs of rejection throughout her married life. God saw Leah's pain and opened her womb whereas Rachel was still barren.

• **Babies.** Leah found an arena where she could win over Rachel – childbearing. Leah and Rachel's rivalry reached an almost feverish level with Leah, her maidservant Zilpah, Rachel and her maidservant Bilhah as contestants. Even the naming of their children demonstrated their competitive feelings. The chart on the next page tracks how the sisters kept score.

By the actual numbers of children born, it looks as if Leah won the baby-making contest, but Jacob through the years still loved Rachel best. Although Leah thought she might gain the upper hand in Jacob's love by providing more sons, his heart still belonged to Rachel.

The truth is that no one wins when women compete like this. Gains

Mother	Child	Comments from Rachel and Leah	Score
Leah	Reuben	"[T]he LORD has seen my misery. Surely my husband will love me now" (Genesis 29:32).	1 – Leah
Leah	Simeon	"Because the LORD heard that I am not loved, he gave me this one too" (v. 33).	1 – Leah
Leah	Levi	"Now at last my husband will become attached to me, because I have borne him three sons." (v. 34).	1 – Leah
Leah	Judah	"This time I will praise the LORD" (v. 35).	1 – Leah
Bilhah	Dan	"God has vindicated me; he has listened to my plea and given me a son' (Genesis 30:6).	1 – Rachel
Bilhah	Naphtali	"I have had a great struggle with my sister, and I have won" (v. 8).	1 – Rachel
Zilpah	Gad	"What good fortune!" (v. 11).	1 – Leah
Zilpah	Asher	"How happy I am! The women will call me happy" (v. 13).	1 – Leah
Leah	Issachar	"God has rewarded me for giving my maidservant to my husband" (v. 18).	1 – Leah
Leah	Zebulun	"God has presented me with a precious gift. This time my husband will treat me with honor, because I have borne him six sons" (v. 20).	1 – Leah
Leah	Dinah	(v. 21)	1 – Leah
Rachel	Joseph	"God has taken away my disgrace … May the LORD add to me another son" (vv. 23-24).	1 – Rachel
Rachel	Benjamin	(35:16-19)	1 – Rachel
			9 – Leah
			4 – Rachel

on one hand are soon overcome by someone else's next triumph. Someone is always smarter, richer, prettier, younger, older or more sophisticated. There is always someone better. The question is not *if* there is someone better. It is *how* we are going to handle it when she eventually appears!

What spawns this spirit of competition? How does it begin? What feeds it and allows it to continue and grow? Should it always be avoided?

Is Competition Always Bad?

Sometime competition can be good. When we compete in sports or sales or Bible bowls, we can be motivated to push a little further or study a little harder. Competition can help girls and women learn to win and lose gracefully. It can help us appreciate someone else's effort and congratulate our opponent on a job well done. Competing as a team can help us learn to work together instead of trying to shine in our own one-person show. That's why many girls find sports, brain squads and other team efforts as healthy outlets in which to compete.

But even these avenues can turn ugly if the will to win goes too far. Much depends on the attitude of those in charge. A sales team can run over each other in cut-throat style, or they can compete against their own best figures and try to improve themselves. It all depends on how the competition is handled.

But how about the day-to-day competition we see every day, such as who has the best-looking boyfriend or best-paying job or most expensive furniture? It seems to start with that bone-rotting disease called envy.

The Bone-Rotting Disease

Envy is wanting what someone else has or feeling bad toward her when she has an advantage. The wise man was right when he wrote, "A heart at peace gives life to the body, but envy rots the bones" (Proverbs 14:30). Envy leaves no room for a peaceful heart because it is never content. Envy is "I wanna" exemplified. It is that uneasy feeling that I am not good enough and so I need to have or be something more. That's the key – the envious person is insecure in what or who she is. When Jesus drew big crowds, the chief priests grew envious of His following among the people. How did they deal with their envy? They killed Him to get Him out of the way (Mark 15:10).

Take envy a step further and it becomes full-fledged jealousy. "I wanna" becomes "I wanna yours!" It is what a little child screams as he takes another's toy away – "MINE!" Joseph's brothers grew jealous of the dreamer who wore the beautiful coat, lovingly crafted by their father Jacob just for him (Genesis 37:11). When the brothers had the opportunity, they sold Joseph into slavery. Then they dipped the coat in goat's blood and took the symbolic object of their jealousy back to their father.

Jealousy taken to its deepest level leads to rivalry, fury, revenge, strife and murder, and it is connected to all kinds of evil (Proverbs 6:34; Romans 13:13; Galatians 5:19-21). King Saul grew resentful of David's military success and acclaim among the people. "And from that time on Saul kept a jealous eye on David" (1 Samuel 18:9). In fact, Saul tried several ways to kill him, eventually playing a competitive cat-and-mouse game with David through the wilderness.

It is sad to note that in all the examples above, envy led to murder or the desire to murder the envied one! Truly envy and its companions, jealousy and rivalry, are serious business! Unfortunately, their roots are often close to home.

Family Roots

The rivalry between Leah and Rachel gives a new dimension to the term "sibling rivalry." Adult competition often comes from family roots, and the impact that Leah and Rachel's family had on their competitive circumstances is undeniable, particularly from their father, Laban. By his trickery, these daughters were set up for a lifetime of potential misery. They could have chosen to act differently, but instead they chose the way of strife and jealousy. They seemed to harbor bitter feelings toward their father when, along with Jacob, they planned to deceive Laban by secretly leaving. Leah and Rachel told Jacob, speaking of Laban, "Does he not regard us as foreigners? Not only has he sold us, but he has used up what was paid for us" (Genesis 31:15). This seemed to be one of the few times in Scripture that we know the two sisters agreed!

Just like Rachel and Leah, women today are deeply affected by how their parents handle sibling rivalry. It is the child's perception of equal and fair treatment by her parents that greatly impacts her relationships with others.

Sometimes parents can even fan the flame of competition by favoring one child over another. This favoritism begins an endless cycle of comparison that creates a ripe breeding ground for envy and jealousy. When Jacob favored Joseph, the son of his favorite wife Rachel, Jacob was carrying on the cycle of what he had known all his life – he was his mother Rebekah's favorite (Genesis 25:28)!

Sometimes it is the mother who is envious of the daughter. A former beauty, now a frumpy middle-aged mother, does not want her lovely teenage daughter to have prettier clothes than she had. Or on the other hand, a shy daughter might get jealous of her mother's exciting social life. A mother and daughter can vie competitively as much as or more than any athlete!

Getting at the Root

There are some things we can do to get at the root of the competition problem:

• **Awareness of the past.** If we take some time to look at our early upbringing, we can try to understand how the dynamics of our family relationships worked. Sometimes we may find that we are repeating destructive cycles of the past that we need to stop. Through reflection on our past, we might even discover solutions to some problems of envy, jealousy and competition with our current family and friends. For instance, a woman always seemed to get jealous when a good friend succeeded. She finally figured out that it was a reminder of the early sibling rivalry with her popular sister. When she dealt with her past, she then found it easier to accept her friend's success.

• **Acceptance of the person.** Acceptance begins with one's self. If mothers can learn to accept themselves first, then they will be more likely to create a climate for self-acceptance in their daughters. Mothers should learn to live their own lives and not live their lives through their daughters. If a daughter feels loved and accepted herself, she can better appreciate the success of others.[6]

• **Appreciation of the possibilities.** As daughters, we understand how parents are in a unique position to bring out the best or worst in their children. Parents can offer an appreciation of all the possibilities open to their daughters. When a daughter is able to try different activities and feels she has several choices in her life of what she can do or be, she will have more opportunities to succeed. Success breeds confidence, which gives her less reason to envy others. A daughter who finds her passion in art, sports, scholastic achievement or whatever it might be is less likely to feel inadequate when compared to someone else.

It's Our Choice

It is interesting to note that hundreds of years later, the Mosaic Law forbade sisters marrying the same man. "Do not take your wife's sister as a rival wife and have sexual relations with her while your wife is living" (Leviticus 18:18). That law was too late to spare Rachel and Leah the grief of endless competition.

But the rationale behind forbidding rivalry between any women is not too late for us to embrace! We do not have to look at any other woman as a rival for any reason. It is ultimately up to us. We can choose to resent and envy others, or we can choose to look at others and ourselves with a godly perspective. "Each one should test his own actions. Then he can take pride in himself, without comparing himself to somebody else, for each one should carry his own load" (Galatians 6:4-5). We can learn to affirm others and their talents and, at the same time, appreciate our own. Which will you choose?

Searching Further

1. What are some possible meanings for Leah's "weak eyes"? How did she compare in beauty to Rachel?

2. How were Jacob and Rachel related? What was the *mohar*? What did Jacob have to do instead to marry Rachel? What happened on his wedding night? Why did he have to work longer?

3. What is a possible explanation why Rachel wanted Leah's mandrakes? Why did God open Leah's womb? Why did He eventually open Rachel's womb?

4. How many children did Leah have? How many children did Zilpah have with Jacob? How many children did Rachel have? How many children did Bilhah have with Jacob?

5. How can competition be beneficial? How can it turn ugly?

6. What is the difference between envy and jealousy? What are some examples in the Bible of each? What can envy and jealousy lead to?

7. How did Laban set his daughters up for rivalry? What do parents do today to fan the flame of unhealthy competition in their children?

8. How did Jacob create a climate for jealousy by his favoritism? Which parent did the same with Jacob?

9. How does being aware of our past make it easier to understand the dynamics of competition in our adult lives?

10. How does acceptance of ourselves and appreciation of others' abilities make us less likely to feel envious of them?

Who Else?

What other two daughters deceived their father (Genesis 19:30-38)?

Safari Savvy

Squelching the Green-Eyed Monster

Jealousy has been called the green-eyed monster. It rips apart the best of friends and rears its ugly head in a multitude of ways. No wonder Solomon wrote: "Anger is cruel and fury overwhelming, but who can stand before jealousy?" (Proverbs 27:4). Jealousy topples many a friendship.

For example, your friend rushes in, talking excitedly about her shiny new car. You have been struggling for months just to save the cash to get your old clunker fixed. Your knee-jerk reaction might be to excuse yourself and head the other way. Instead, ask yourself: Am I being too sensitive? Does her good news make me feel like a loser, when I really am not? Use this as an opportunity to count your talents and blessings. When you remember how God has blessed you, it makes it easier to appreciate others' blessings.

Turn the tables for a minute. How would you want your friend to react if you had good news? Although it might be difficult, try to be happy for her, just like you would want her to be happy for you. If she goes on and on, you might tactfully change the subject. If she still does not get the message, you might use her news as a bridge to another topic, "Speaking of gas mileage, do you think gas prices will ever go down?" or "I'm thrilled at your good news. Why don't you take me on a test drive to the new store at the mall?"

Friendships can be strained by trials and crises, but they are even more tested when one friend seems more successful. Bette Midler observed, "The worst part of success is to try to find someone who is happy for you."[7] It takes a special friendship to find the balance between sharing and empathy, honesty and sensitivity. These qualities have the potential power to squelch any monster – even a green-eyed one![8]

Chapter 10

Hanging on for Dear Life

I magine how it would feel to be swinging on a jungle vine, the world below dizzily passing you by. Would you feel ecstatic to see such a marvelous view? Or would you feel weightless as you swirled along at such a speed? Possibly you might feel terrified to be so high above the jungle floor and hanging on for dear life!

One woman long ago was hanging on for dear life. It was as if her jungle vine had ripped off, sending her plummeting below, broken and bitter. She felt too tired and old to pick up the pieces. She felt she had lost everything and everyone dear to her. It took another woman – a friend – to help her find her life again.

Moving to Moab and Back

If you had to move and take everything you had, what would it take to haul it away? A pickup truck? A moving van? Three moving vans?

In the book of Ruth, Naomi did not have the luxury of calling up Moabite Movers Camel Caravan ("You stack 'em, We pack 'em") to pack up her stuff. It seemed she did not have enough worldly goods left to make it worth their while. Her life was empty. From what we can tell, all she had left she moved herself (Ruth 1:6-7).

She had not started out that way. Her life had been full with her husband, Elimelech, and her two sons, Mahlon and Kilion. When famine had swept through their home in Bethlehem, Elimelech felt it wise to move to more fertile fields in Moab. There the sons met and married two Moabite women, Ruth and Orpah.

Then things began to go wrong. First Elimelech then Mahlon and Kilion died in Moab. It was difficult enough to be without a man at home, but her emptiness seemed magnified in a foreign country. When she heard the famine was over in Bethlehem, she wanted to go home. Although Ruth and Orpah did not have to follow Naomi, they initially joined her in the journey back to Bethlehem, no doubt due to their fondness for her.[1]

After they set out, Naomi thought of their own welfare and urged them to go back to their mothers' homes. Although it was customary for a father to protect his family, it was usually the mother who found a husband for her daughter. If Ruth and Orpah were to marry again, they would need to go back to their mothers. Naomi blessed and kissed her daughters-in-law goodbye, but they refused to go back. She reasoned that even if she had other sons, they would be too young for them to marry. Finally Orpah left and headed back to Moab.

However, Ruth clung to Naomi. Perhaps Ruth could see beyond the bitter old woman. Maybe she remembered the former Naomi and had seen what grief and hardship had done to her. Ruth knew that a widow without a male protector would be in a desperate situation, much like a homeless person today.[2] Ruth made a pledge to stay with Naomi whatever came their way.

Despite the danger involved for two women traveling alone, Naomi and Ruth made the week-long trip of approximately 70 to 100 miles to Bethlehem.[3, 4] When they arrived in this small Judean town (most likely with a population of fewer than 200), the women there were abuzz with the question, "Can this be Naomi?" (Ruth 1:19).[5] Were they so overjoyed at her sudden appearance, or had she changed so much that they hardly recognized her?[6] Naomi told them that the name "Naomi," which meant "pleasant," was no longer appropriate. They could now call her "Mara," meaning "bitter" (v. 20). Naomi followed the custom of changing her name to show a life-changing event or transition in her life.[7] But her life was soon to change again because of Ruth's friendship!

Accepting and Staying

Although Naomi and Ruth had been related by marriage, they wove a deeper bond based on trust, companionship and kindness. Ruth (whose name traditionally meant "friend" or "friendship") knew what it means to be a true friend – accepting someone for who she is and staying by her whatever happens.[8] She was willing to glean in the fields for the leftovers of grain after the workers had cut and bound the sheaves. This work spared Naomi the humiliation and exhausting labor involved and also provided food for the two of them.[9] Ruth served as the daughter she never had. Naomi, in turn, served as a mother to Ruth by helping her find her husband, Boaz. It was usually the mother who supervised her daughter in the affairs of the heart such as love, marriage and sex. When Naomi suggested a course of action to claim Boaz as a kinsman-redeemer, Ruth wholeheartedly followed.

After the marriage of Ruth and Boaz, a son named Obed was born to the couple. Naomi's joy was complete again. Speaking to Naomi, the women of Bethlehem praised Ruth for her steadfastness: "For your daughter-in-law, who loves you and who is better to you than seven sons, has given him birth" (Ruth 4:15). This commendation is extraordinary considering that sons were thought to be so much more valuable than daughters at that time.[10]

Ultimately both Ruth and Naomi were blessed in their relationship, and their friendship served as a blessing for years to come. Obed was the father of Jesse, who was the father of King David. So Ruth was a great-grandmother many times over of our Lord and Savior Jesus Christ! Who would have thought that a friendship between two women could be so important?

Accepting Our Differences

When we look at the friendship between Naomi and Ruth, we long for relationships like theirs in which women accept each other wholeheartedly. But just as it did then, accepting others means taking risks. It would have been easy for Ruth to head home to the familiar life she knew, but instead she reached out and welcomed Naomi, despite their differences, to forge a deeper friendship together.

A lot of our relational problems with other women stem from our inability to accept their differences. Perhaps we think deep down inside that if everyone were more like us, the world would be a better place! The truth is that we cannot all be exactly alike, and we would not want to be. The world would be a terribly boring place if we were carbon copies of each other.

Paul told the Christians in Rome, "Accept one another, then, just as Christ accepted you, in order to bring praise to God" (Romans 15:7). The idea behind the Greek word "accept" is to "receive" and "welcome."[11] In that context, Paul was speaking to a diverse audience of Jews and Gentiles who grew up despising each other. Some had notoriously sinful backgrounds. If Jesus accepted them, are we too good to follow His example and accept those who are different from us?

We are all different. God made us that way. Sometimes we think other women are interesting. Sometimes they are eccentric. And sometimes they seem just plain weird! Whatever we think of them, the Lord loves them, and they need our love. He accepts them, and so should we. Women are longing just to be accepted. If women could feel safe to be themselves, then they would not have to put on a facade. They would not have to be afraid that no one would like them for who they are.

Accepting others and being friendly to them means that we need to be vulnerable and open so that they can see we are genuine. That vulnerability can be scary at times. It can mean risking rejection. Many women will respond to your friendliness; but if they do not, the Lord will know you tried. In the process, you might have gained a friend or two or more.

Some women give up on friendship entirely because of relationships that have gone sour. We need to remember that even Jesus and Paul were rejected. Paul wrote poignantly to the Corinthians, "We have spoken freely to you, Corinthians, and opened wide our hearts to you. We are not withholding our affection from you, but you are withholding yours from us. As a fair exchange – I speak as to my children – open wide your hearts also" (2 Corinthians 6:11-13). We need to open wide our hearts to others. That is the only way to have true, heartfelt friendships.[12]

Filled With Memories or Regrets?

When we are old, we want to look back at fond memories of our friends. It is now that we are making those memories. Will those memories be sweet or filled with regrets? To make them sweet, we can take steps to develop memorable friendships that are worth holding on to.

• **Encourage**. We need to move beyond envy and jealousy to wish other women well. Paul wrote, "Therefore encourage one another and build each other up, just as in fact you are doing" (1 Thessalonians 5:11). Encouraging and building up involves support, prayer and genuine compliments when appropriate.

Although it means a lot to a woman to receive a compliment on her new dress or stylish haircut, it would mean even more to be appreciated for her specific inner qualities. These characteristics often go unnoticed, but they are an intrinsic part of who she is, her own personal identity. Think how you would feel if another woman expressed these thoughts to you:

"You are always so cheerful. Your smile lights up the room."

"I know it wasn't easy to stand up for her like you did. That took a lot of courage."

"You have such a giving heart."

"You really worked hard on that. It shows!"[13]

• **Initiate**. It is so easy to think, "I'll let her ask me first" or "It's her turn to ask me." Why wait on someone else to act and let a friendship never happen or slip away? Wouldn't it be better to take action and feel as if you made an effort? If someone doesn't respond positively, you can try again later or move on to someone else. Take the plunge and introduce yourself to your new neighbor or co-worker. Make the call. Send a card. Get the e-mail address and send a note. Get together with a school buddy you have not seen in years. Start a group of ladies who get together with common interests in a "Lunch Bunch." We never know when the woman we contact will become a good friend!

• **Be devoted**. Devote yourself to your friendships. So often we say, "Well, I am not going to invest my time and energy into this friendship because it might not last." How do we know unless we try? It is true that a friendship may not last a lifetime. It might not even make it a week! Enjoy the friendship for the moment. However long it lasts, it will have served a purpose, and you both will be richer for the experience.

It has been said that friends first connect with common interests and "hang out" together. If the friendship continues, they help each other in crises and "hang in" there for each other. If they survive crises together, they "hang on" to one another as true friends.[14] As Walker Percy stated, "We love those who know the worst of us and don't turn their faces away."[15] May God bless us with friends we can hold on to and who will not turn their faces away!

Searching Further

1. What happened in Naomi's life that made her feel empty and bitter?

2. Why did Naomi encourage Ruth and Orpah to go back to their mothers' houses? Who left Naomi? Who stayed with her?

3. How far was the journey from Moab to Bethlehem? About how long did it take? What do you think made it dangerous for two single women?

4. What did the women say to Naomi when she arrived in Bethlehem? Why?

5. What did Naomi's name mean? What was her new name, and what did it mean? What did Ruth's name mean traditionally?

6. How did Ruth and Naomi help each other in Bethlehem? Whom did Ruth meet and marry? What was their son's name? What connection did Ruth have with David and Christ?

7. What is the idea behind the Greek word "accept" in Romans 15:7? How does its meaning translate into our lives today in dealing with other women?

8. What are some ways we can let other women know we appreciate their inner qualities?

9. Why is it important that we each make the first move toward friendship?

10. Why are we so hesitant to invest time and energy into some friendships? Can even short-term friendships serve a purpose?

Who Else?

Who else had a name change (Genesis 17:15)?

Circles of Friends

Ruth did not know it, but when she cast her lot with Naomi, she found more than a friend – she found community. The women of Bethlehem became a ready-made welcoming committee as they surrounded Ruth and Naomi and later baby Obed. This group filled a lonely void in the hearts of the two widows.

Today we need community just like Ruth and Naomi. Although one-on-one friendships are vital, they do not fill the same role as community. Whether it is called a tribe, clan or gang, groups accept us as members and anchor us. In the past, women easily found a group at the neighborhood sewing circle or quilting bee. Today it is more difficult as we hurtle along with our rushed lifestyles and complicated schedules. Even if we are not "joiners," we often feel untethered if we are not part of a group somewhere.

Boston College professor Belle Liang has found that women who hang out with a group tend to be less anxious, depressed and lonely. She sees a circle of friends in some ways more important than individual friends because they help a woman feel grounded in something bigger than herself.[16] Such groups might focus on interests as diverse as Bible study, biking, books, flowers, sewing, walking, international cooking, hang gliding, speech making or scrapbooking.

We might think of our friendships forming concentric circles: an inner ring of our closest friends to understand our deepest feelings, then outer bands of social groups and casual friends to offer a sense of belonging and companionship. Each has a place in our circles of friends. "Do not forsake your friend and the friend of your father, and do not go to your brother's house when disaster strikes you – better a neighbor nearby than a brother far away" (Proverbs 27:10).

Chapter 11

Playing Games of Power

A nimals in the jungle play games of power every day. They must demonstrate who is the strongest, fastest, even the most patient. For in the world they live in, only the strongest or the fastest or the most patient animal survives.

Women play games of power too. They played them in ancient times, and they continue to play them today. Throughout the history of our principally male-dominated society, some women have grabbed for power whenever and wherever they could get it, sometimes with surprising and long-reaching results.

If there were any woman in the Bible involved in power games, it seems the last one we would think of would be Sarah. Sarah was commended in 1 Peter 3:6 for being submissive to Abraham and for calling her husband master and lord. In fact, she obeyed him to the extreme of lying about their husband/wife relationship when he was afraid that foreign men would kill him to marry her (Genesis 12:13; 20:2, 13).

Yet Sarah had a darker side. Genesis 16 and 21 reveal that she played power games with another woman she could control. Why did Sarah act that way, and how we can avoid playing the same games?

Power, Sex and Misery

A woman today might feel a slave to her job, but she does not expect sex with her boss to be part of the job description! Yet in Bible times, if a slave woman or bondswoman were the property of the wife, she could be expected to bear the children of her master. Her children could have the full rights of any children born to his wife. She was considered property and a legal extension of her mistress.[1] Jacob's children, for example, were all treated equally under the Law, although some were born through Rachel's handmaiden (Bilhah) and Leah's handmaiden (Zilpah).[2]

Likewise, when Sarah was childless and past her childbearing prime, she gave her personal slave Hagar to Abraham to be his wife and to have his children. This transferal in essence put Hagar in Abraham's control rather than Sarah's.

When Hagar got pregnant, she grew to despise Sarah. Before Hagar became Abraham's wife, she was just a slave. Now she had something her mistress had never had – a child. Women at that time derived much of their honor from marriage and children, and Hagar made the most of her elevated situation. It is possible she even felt she should replace Sarah (Proverbs 30:21-23)! An already frustrated Sarah unfairly blamed Abraham for the situation *she* had initiated.

Abraham put Hagar under Sarah's authority again, which gave Sarah the power to discipline her.[3] We do not know if her abuse was physical, psychological or both, but her mistreatment was so severe that Hagar ran away to escape. In the desert of Shur, possibly on Hagar's way back home to Egypt, an angel told her to go back to Sarah, for the son Hagar was carrying would grow up to become the father of numerous descendants. With renewed hope, she returned to Sarah and had her son, Ishmael, when Abraham was 86 years old. No doubt Ishmael brought Hagar joy, although her relationship with Sarah most likely did not.

About 14 years later, the promised son Isaac was born to Sarah. When Isaac was about 2 or 3 years old, a feast celebrating his weaning was held. At this special occasion, Ishmael mocked his baby half-brother. This infuriated Sarah, and she demanded that Abraham send Hagar and her son away. Sarah did not want Ishmael to share in the inheritance with Isaac. Although Abraham was attached to his son, God in a dream told him to expel the two of them because Ishmael would make a great nation too. So Abraham sent Hagar and Ishmael off to fend for themselves in the desert with what they could carry – bread and water.

Once again, Hagar found herself in the desert with little food, water and less hope. After she had given her teenage son the last drink of water, she sat down some distance away so as not to see him die. God caused Hagar to see the well before them. He also predicted that Ishmael would live and become a great nation. Not only did both she and her son live, but Hagar also obtained something very precious when she left Abraham's household – her freedom!

Let the Power Games End

In the relationship of Sarah and Hagar lie a myriad of power issues. We see wives fighting for status in bearing children (Genesis 16:4). We also see mothers fighting for their sons' inheritance (21:10). We even see women jealous over the attention of their husband (16:5). What is unique in their conflict is the employer/employee relationship. What gave Sarah the power to tell Abraham to dismiss Hagar and send her and her son packing into the desert, essentially to die? Hagar was the slave, and Sarah was the mistress.

Power issues were what seemed to be the problem in Sarah and Hagar's relationship. Sarah felt powerless to have a child. Hagar felt powerless as a slave. No wonder Sarah felt angry and threatened when Hagar knew she was pregnant. As mother of Abraham's child, Hagar probably felt more power and status than she had felt before. And Sarah herself had given Hagar that power!

Trampling on Women to Succeed

Although Sarah's and Hagar's lives were quite different from ours today, we too experience power issues in our relationships with other women, especially in any situation where women work together. This includes the company board or the school board, the university committee or the women's church committee. Wherever women work, they often find themselves working side by side with other women.

In the workplace, more women are in positions of authority than ever before. But many women still feel limited by the glass ceiling, that invisible roof that prevents them from getting promotions and benefits that their male co-workers seem to enjoy. When women get the chance to get ahead, some feel the need to step on other women to climb the ladder of success. They fear that other women will take their jobs, their promotions and their success. So who is often the worst competition in a woman's workplace? Other women![4]

A woman can undermine other women in many ways whenever and wherever they work together – whether it is the downtown office or downstairs home office. Women use different tactics in their power games:

• **The Bully Boss.** The game plan for the Bully Boss is intimidation. This type of bully makes the victim feel incompetent and unworthy in her job. The Bully Boss antagonizes a worker by constantly or harshly criticizing or insulting her and discounting her opinions and contributions. This kind of boss sets up the worker to fail by denying necessary resources, equipment and training. She may even invade her victim's office space, memos and e-mails.

• **The Sneaky Subordinate.** The name of the game for the Sneaky Subordinate is sabotage. The woman manager finds her work much more difficult when she supervises a woman who sabotages her authority. The Sneaky Subordinate undermines her manager's authority by belittling her opinions and requests, using disrespectful language to describe her, and twisting information to make the boss look bad.

• **The Competitive Co-worker.** "Withholding" is the Competitive Co-worker's byword. She withholds information regarding work or office activities and encourages others to snub the co-worker. She tries to get the competitive edge over anyone who threatens her. She might use the silent treatment to alienate a co-worker or stare, glare, roll her eyes or use other negative eye contact.[5]

Do We Have to Play Their Games?

Clearly, we do not have to play the games of power some women play. Instead we can prepare ourselves to reverse the way some women think. Instead of the love of power, we can show them the greatest power that only God provides – the power of love – through his Son, Jesus Christ.

Jesus' life was the epitome of the power of love overcoming the love of power. Although death and the devil had tremendous power over mankind, making us powerless, Christ overcame them both by dying on the cross for us (Romans 5:6-8). In that great redeeming act of love, He showed us the true meaning of the power of love. He asks us to do the same in our relationships with people.

In the Sermon on the Mount, Christ gave us a succinct principle for dealing with others: love your enemies as well as your friends (Matthew 5:43-47). Those enemies might not be likeable. They might even hate you and be mean to you. But Jesus commanded us to love them anyway. The path to real maturity means that we love them in the true sense of the word. In this context, the Greek word for "love" is the verb *agapao*, which refers to a love rooted in the will and mind. This love means to be devoted to, esteem, prize, value, cherish, honor, favor, respect and accept.[6]

But how does that definition translate to everyday life and to power struggles both in and out of the workplace? How are we to cherish the competitive co-worker who gossips about us, respect the power-hungry committee chairwoman who bullies us, and prize the snobby neighbor who snubs us? Even on our best days, those are a tall order!

Paul helps us by defining what love does. Love truly is an action word. It can be defined as an emotion in motion. Its description in 1 Corinthians 13:4-7 transfers well to our daily walk with other women who play power games. Love dictates how we act despite what others do:

• "Love is patient" when a boring relative monopolizes the conversation.

• "Love is kind" when a rude bank teller snaps at us.

• "It does not envy" when a committee member shows off her new house.

• "It does not boast" when our in-law will not quit bragging about her son.

• "It is not proud" when a co-worker boasts about her musical talent.

• "It is not rude" when a friend drones on about her ailments.

• "It is not self-seeking" when team members think only of themselves.

• "It is not easily angered" when a coach challenges us to verbally spar with her.

• "It keeps no record of wrongs" when a boss keeps score of our mistakes.

- "Love does not delight in evil but rejoices in the truth" when a neighbor downplays and laughs at the decadence in our society.

Love Wins

Although Jesus' directive to love is sometimes difficult to put into practice, it makes an incredible difference in the ways we deal with women every day. Women wonder why we act differently than others who play power games. In reality, we "win" the power game because ultimately love wins over power! The Christian's power is in love. As Paul wrote to Timothy, "For God did not give us a spirit of timidity, but a spirit of power, of love and of self-discipline" (2 Timothy 1:7). The power of love will triumph over the love of power. Let's start today to make it happen!

Searching Further

1. How was Sarah commended in 1 Peter 3:6? Was Abraham asking Sarah to lie when he asked her to say she was his sister? What motive does he give for asking her to do this? How does this scripture imply that she might have told this story more than the two times recorded (Genesis 20:13)?

2. How did Paul use the analogy of Sarah, Hagar, Ishmael and Isaac to illustrate the difference between the old and new Laws (Romans 9:6-9; Galatians 4:21-31)? What word does Paul use in Galatians 4:29 to describe Ishmael's treatment of Isaac?

3. Why could a master sometimes expect his slaves or bondswomen to bear his children? Were all his children treated equally under the Law? Why did Abraham resort to this scheme?

4. Why did Hagar grow to despise Sarah? How did Sarah retaliate? How did the angel intervene? What promise did Hagar receive from the angel?

5. What did Ishmael do at Isaac's weaning party? How did Sarah react? What did God tell Abraham to do? How did God intervene again in the desert?

6. What are some of the power issues that Sarah and Hagar dealt with in their relationship? Why did Sarah feel as if she had the upper hand? How did God ultimately control the situation?

7. Why have women throughout the ages felt powerless? Why do they especially feel less power in the workplace? How do some women compensate for their lack of power over men?

8. What are three tactics that some women use to undermine other women in the workplace?

9. Who shows us how the power of love can triumph over the love of power?

10. What are some practical examples of how the real meaning of love dictates how we act despite what others do (1 Corinthians 13:4-7)?

Who Else?

Who else provoked another member of her household (1 Samuel 1:6-7)?

Safari Savvy
Keeping in Touch

Just like all living things, friendships need tending if they are to thrive. They must be nurtured. If we do not keep in touch, we risk losing relationships that might have taken years to cultivate. But how do we show we care?

We can begin by introducing our friends to each other to create a growing network of women who can enjoy and benefit from each other's company. Some women periodically have a potluck where everyone brings a new person and a new dish. Others plan a game night for cards or board games with an open invitation for friends to bring their friends.

Although it is not always easy, be upfront with your friends about your feelings and be willing to listen to theirs. Ask for their opinions and advice. Even if you do not agree with them, you can gain different perspectives from people you value. "Perfume and incense bring joy to the heart, and the pleasantness of one's friend springs from his earnest counsel" (Proverbs 27:9). Be honest about your fears and insecurities. Let them know you are human. Don't be afraid to say "I'm wrong" or "I'm sorry."

Show your friends appreciation for what they do. Send them notes and cards to let them know you are thinking of them. Remember what piques their enthusiasm. Send them magazine or Internet articles that they might find helpful or interesting. Pay attention to their likes and dislikes. Be on the lookout for little gifts to brighten their day.

Utilize a mind-tickler system so you won't forget birthdays, anniversaries and other days to remember. Find novel ways to celebrate the special times (and ordinary times) in your friends' lives. Celebrate their friendship for the precious gift it is![7]

Chapter 12

Yodeling and Other Jungle Communication

When Tarzan needed to communicate with his animal friends, he did what every self-respecting man of the jungle would do – he yodeled! His eclectic mixture of high and low vocal tones brought animals from all corners of the jungle stampeding to his side. Their response to his cry of help was immediate and unmistakable.

If only our communication with people could be that effective! Yodeling might work in fiction; but in our real world, we sometimes struggle to get our *family* to really listen, much less get a response from a friend, co-worker or woman on the street. Often they do not have the time or are too busy thinking of what they want to say next.

The truth is that communication is more than just talking and listening. It involves what you meant to say, what you actually said, what the other person heard, what the other person thinks she heard, and what the other person says about what you said.[1]

Women usually talk more than men, so it would seem we should have the nuances of communication down to a science. Instead we have difficulty saying how we actually feel. In our effort to be nice and not hurt anyone's feelings, we sometimes betray ourselves. Instead of speaking directly to one another, we communicate indirectly by words or actions and then hope our hearers understand what we were trying to say. Or we hold our true feelings in, and eventually they spill out like a torrential downpour of hurtful words. In Luke 10:38-42, we are told about one woman who communicated in just this way.

Flustered and Frustrated

Martha was bumfuzzled! She was flustered and frustrated. She had opened her home to friends – at least 13, in fact – and was bustling around trying to take care of all the details. These guests were not just anyone; they were Jesus and His disciples. She wanted everything to be just right, but she needed help. Over there was her sister Mary just sitting at Jesus' feet and listening to Him! How was Martha supposed to get everything done? If we were in Martha's sandals, we might be bumfuzzled too!

After Martha felt she could not take it any longer, she unloaded on Jesus, "Lord, don't you care that my sister has left me to do the work by myself? Tell her to help me!" (Luke 10:40). Jesus gently chided Martha for being distracted by the preparation for their physical nourishment while Mary chose the more important spiritual food "spread" at His feet.

We wonder if Martha had asked her sister to help her. Had she told her sister how frustrated she felt? In the crush of responsibilities upon her, perhaps she did not take the time. Perhaps Martha assumed Mary would join her in the preparations. Or maybe Martha did ask Mary to help, but Mary became engrossed in what the Lord was saying and lost track of time – and Martha's growing irritation. Although it is possible that Martha had asked Mary to help before, it is not recorded in Scripture.

In the graphic scene that Luke paints for us, we see Martha communicating like many of us. Maybe she didn't want to seem like a "mean sister" and scold Mary. Perhaps Martha didn't feel comfortable in taking Mary aside and interrupting the Lord's teaching. So she let her frustration mount until she spoke indirectly *about* Mary's action *to* someone else.

How many times have we done the same thing? We let our irritation grow until we can no longer hold our tongue. Or perhaps when a friend makes us angry, we resort to pouting or clamming up instead of airing our concern? Or maybe we act as if nothing is wrong – when in reality something is wrong. It is true that it is not always possible or wise to discuss every problem we have with the person who is causing it. But how much better our relationships would be if we could talk with each other openly to understand and work out the things that can drive us apart.

Keys to Communication

So how do we communicate with other women in our day-to-day conversations? Are we usually direct or indirect? We might think of a woman who speaks directly as being rude, pushy or unfeminine, but she does not have to be that way. We can be honest without being rude, and we can be direct without seeming pushy. If we look to Jesus for our example, we can learn to communicate more effectively with other women.

• **Genuinely listening.** Sometimes we forget that listening is an important key to effective communication. Because we like to talk so much, we are often so eager to speak that we hardly let the other person finish. As the wise man wrote, "He who answers before listening – that is his folly and his shame" (Proverbs 18:13).

Listening is crucial in getting along and communicating with other women. By listening, we just might learn something, like the wise owl:

> A wise old owl lived in an oak;
> The more he saw, the less he spoke;
> The less he spoke, the more he heard;
> Why can't we all be like that bird?[2]

By listening, you have a better chance to understand what the other woman is really thinking. You can then guide the flow and direction of the conversation by the questions you ask and the statements you make. When you show by your body language that you are listening, the other woman feels more comfortable to keep talking.[3]

Genuinely listening was one way Jesus demonstrated His love and concern to those who spoke with Him. By listening to the Samaritan woman's questions, the Lord was able to draw her out. He then was able to satisfy her curiosity and thirst for spiritual things (John 4:1-26).

• **Thinking about our response.** We as Christian women have learned civility too well. We say we would be glad to help others when in reality we do not even want to think of adding one more item to our "to do" list. We say we don't mind pitching in when we really do mind. If we just automatically give in or go along to get along, we will either resent fulfilling our commitment or back out, causing the person who asked us to resent us.[4] So either way is toxic for relationships.

James tells us, "Everyone should be quick to listen, slow to speak and slow to become angry" (James 1:19). When we are asked to do something we are not sure we can handle, we need to slow down and think before we speak. It is a commendable urge to want to help, but it is better for everyone if we first conduct an internal check: what will this activity cost in effort, money and time? We may need to ask for more information or ask for more time before we make a decision. If you can handle the request, fine. But if you cannot, it is better to say directly, "I'm overwhelmed right now, and I will not have the time" or "That just won't be convenient for me."[5]

Saying "no" does seem to contradict the "servant mentality" of Christianity. Are we not supposed to deny ourselves and help others? It is true that Christ challenges us to be giving people. But Jesus Himself set boundaries on His time, energy and ministry, and so should we. We see our Lord balancing between time alone and time with people, healing and teaching the crowds and socializing and relaxing with friends. For example, when Jesus had left the house to pray alone early one morning, Simon and His other companions discovered He was missing and went to look for Him. When they found Him, they told Jesus that everyone was looking for Him. Instead of going with them, however, He replied that He needed to go elsewhere to teach others (Mark 1:35-39). During His time on earth, Jesus could not be everywhere at once, and neither can we.

• **Volleying rude questions.** We wonder where some women get the audacity to say what they say! Some of their comments are totally rude, intrusive and inappropriate. There are three general ways to handle harsh comments directly:

(1) *Silence.* Some rude, nosey questions do not deserve an answer. Silence, sometimes with pointed eye contact with the inquisitor, speaks volumes. Usually this encourages the woman to realize that she has gone too far, back off and maybe even apologize. If the request is persistent, you can even reply, "I don't feel comfortable answering that."[6]

When the Jewish leaders came to accuse the woman caught in adultery, Jesus chose to stoop and write on the ground. Their agitation grew, as did the length of His silence. Perhaps He was giving them time to think – in silence – on their manipulative actions (John 8:2-11).

(2) *Another question.* Sometimes it helps to answer a rude question with another question – "Why do you ask?" This response should give you time to think mindfully what, if anything, you want to say next. This response needs to be pleasant, without hostility or sarcasm. Most people will realize that their questions are inappropriate (for example, "How much did you pay for that dress? Is that a real diamond? How much does your husband make? Did you get a nose job?"). Hopefully, they will move on to another topic.[7]

Jesus often answered His critics with another question. Besides catching them off guard, it usually gave them a deeper question to ponder. Once the Lord even told His critics they had to answer His question before He would answer theirs (Mark 11:27-33)!

(3) *Clever answer.* These alternatives can work in answering a boorish woman's question:

Q: "How much money do you make?"

A: "Enough to keep me happy and pay the bills!"

Q: "Is that genuine silver or zirconium?"

A: "I'm really glad you like it!"

Q: "How much do you weigh?"

A: "Do you really think I look that good? Thanks!"[8]

Jesus was the master of the clever repartee, especially when He dealt with the Jewish leaders who thought they were so clever themselves. In a few choice words, He often put them in their place (Mark 12:13-17).

• **Dealing with criticism.** Criticism is difficult to accept. As women, we find it especially hard because we often tend to be less confrontational and have less experience in dealing with criticism than men. Consequently, we avoid or delay it whenever we can.[9]

When we take on new challenges or learn new skills, we are going to make mistakes. Our goal is to learn from these mistakes and react maturely and honestly without being apologetic or defensive. The problem arises when criticism is unjust, untrue, exaggerated or presented in a hostile way. Then we often get hurt or defensive. This reaction keeps us from being objective and acting on the problem. Instead we need to respond to the amount of truth contained in the criticism, whether it is not true, partially true or entirely true.

For example, when a committee chairwoman accuses you of never preparing your reports on time, you can question her about whether every report was late (not true). If a mother criticizes your handling of her child in your Bible class, be sure she hears your side of the story as well as the child's version (partially true). When you sent in the incorrect form, admit you are wrong and go on to ask for suggestions to get it right next time (true).[10]

Jesus certainly had His share of criticism. Some critics came under the guise of learning more about His teaching when actually they were testing Him. Others were obviously rude, almost mocking in nature (John 18:19-23). Jesus handled them all with such agility and wisdom that the common people marveled at His answers. We hope that someday we can handle all our communication as well as He did!

Searching Further

1. Why can communication get complicated? Why do women sometimes have difficulty saying how they truly feel?

2. Why was Martha frustrated? Why do you think she asked the Lord to help? What did the Lord tell her was more important?

3. Does a woman have to be rude to be direct? What are some examples in support of your answer?

4. How can we guide the flow of a conversation by listening? How can we show by our body language that we are interested in hearing more?

5. How can we show how much we care for people by how we listen to them?

6. Why is it wise for us to think before we respond to a request? When did Jesus set boundaries on His time and energy?

7. How can we use silence to answer rude questions? When did the Lord utilize silence when the Jewish leaders came to Him?

8. How can we answer a rude question with another question? When did Christ respond to His critics with a question?

9. Why is criticism often especially difficult for women to accept? What circumstances make it more difficult?

10. What are some examples of ways we can respond to criticism that is not true, partially true, or completely true?

Who Else?

Who else spoke against his/her sibling (Genesis 37:19-20; Numbers 12)?

Safari Savvy
Words of Gold

Silence might be golden, but so are our words – if they are appropriate. "A word aptly spoken is like apples of gold in settings of silver" (Proverbs 25:11). Some words are just more suitable than others to say to a friend.

• **About her size.** Friends are often sensitive about their size. Observing "You've lost tons of weight!" implies she weighed tons before! "Are you pregnant?" could mean that she looks overweight. You might say instead, "You look fantastic!" or just "It's good to see you."[11]

• **About a favor.** A friend would rather be asked than told to do something. Do not assume she can or will automatically drop everything and help you. Give her a choice by asking. Women chafe under brisk orders or assumed expectations, especially when it comes from another woman. "Would you please do this for me?" sounds much better than demanding "Handle it."[12]

• **About her appearance.** Friends care about how they look – or at least they do not like to be told they look like something the cat dragged in! Declaring "You look really tired" to a friend implies that she looks bad. "Is everything alright?" shows concern without putting down her appearance. "I could never wear that" might be misunderstood. (Is it too ugly?) A better choice might be "You look marvelous in that dress." "You look really good for your age" gives the impression that although she is ancient, she is still well preserved! Instead compliment her with "You look lovely!"[13]

Chapter 13

Following
Your Guide

E very adventurer knows the first rule of the jungle: Never go in
alone. This directive is especially true if you are inexperienced
in jungle survival. A guide can not only show you the best routes
but also help you survive if you run into trouble. Occasionally, even a
guide gets lost or faces an emergency. Because she probably has been
there before, she is more likely to get you out alive, safe and sound.

Just like in the jungle, we need a guide who can help us in our relationships. We need someone with whom we can share our concerns,
triumphs, sorrows and joys. It helps if she has experienced what we are
facing. Maybe she has not experienced it, but she is willing to walk beside us as we go through it. Sometimes we just need someone to talk
to or hang out with. One young woman needed all this and more.

Whom Can I Turn To?

Mary was still in awe from the message of the angel Gabriel. This
young woman, probably a teenager, would be the mother of the promised Messiah! Every Jewish woman longed for this honor, and God by
His grace had chosen her! She still wondered how the Holy Spirit would
accomplish it. She was an unmarried Jewish virgin, about 14 years old
or younger.[1] But she took Gabriel at his word.

We can imagine Mary wondering how she could be pregnant without sexual relations. If her situation was difficult for her to understand, how would she explain it to other people? Who would believe her? If they did not, they could accuse her of adultery, punishable by stoning (Deuteronomy 22:23-29).

More importantly, would her fiancé Joseph believe her? Joseph could legally divorce her when he considered the possibility of scandal as her pregnancy became public.[2] In fact, he would have divorced her if it had not been for a message from the angel (Matthew 1:18-25). In those days, betrothals usually lasted a year and were as binding as marriage and only broken by divorce.[3]

Perhaps Mary remembered Gabriel's words again, "Even Elizabeth your relative is going to have a child in her old age, and she who was said to be barren is in her sixth month" (Luke 1:36). Of all people, Elizabeth would understand what was happening to Mary. So Mary hurried to the hill country of Judea where Elizabeth lived. She might have made the 3-5 day journey by herself, but no doubt her parents preferred that she join herself to a caravan traveling in that direction.[4]

When she arrived at Elizabeth's house, Mary greeted her friend. At that moment, Elizabeth felt her own baby leap in her womb. Filled with the Holy Spirit, Elizabeth blessed Mary and her baby. Mary had found a kindred spirit and caring confidant in Elizabeth. The younger mother stayed with Elizabeth for about three months, probably long enough to be with Elizabeth when John was born. What a happy day that was for both mothers!

A Supporting Role

If anyone needed support in what she would be facing, it was Mary. The Lord provided Elizabeth, who was in a unique position as an older woman but also as a new mother. Can you imagine the giggling between this gray-haired matron and the budding young teenager, both new to pregnancy?

It is not surprising that these relatives, so different in some ways, could offer each other so much. Elizabeth was barren and older, "well along in years" (Luke 1:7, 18). Mary was probably at the beginning of her childbearing age, eventually having at least seven children (Matthew 13:55-56). Elizabeth enjoyed support from a network of neighbors and relatives (Luke 1:57-58). We do not know how much support Mary received, but the potential negative response could have caused Joseph to want to put her away privately. Elizabeth had probably been married many years. Mary was not only a new mother but also had never known the challenges or blessings of marriage. She needed advice and encouragement to make the many adjustments ahead of her.

Elizabeth served as a valuable mentor to the younger Mary. At the same time, Mary offered Elizabeth precious companionship in this exciting time in their lives. What strength they must have found in each other! What spiritual support they could offer one another!

Older Women Mentoring the Younger

Mary and Elizabeth illustrate the value of a mentoring relationship between an older and a younger woman. Although peer mentoring can be worthwhile for both women, a special richness can be shared between women of different seasons of life. As author Marla Paul relates, "An older friend remembers whether the sandbags worked or if you just have to watch the creek rise. She also knows the waters eventually recede. She can tell you how she survived and even thrived."[5]

Paul advocated this kind of relationship in Titus 2:3-5 when he admonished older women to teach younger women. We are all older and younger than someone else. Yet many older women are hesitant or even resistant to mentor younger women.

There are several reasons why more women do not mentor each other. Our mobile and age-polarized society makes it more difficult to make long-lasting relationships between generations. Age and experience have become devalued whereas youth is applauded. Some younger women exude an independence that says, "I don't need you or anyone else." Some older women feel inadequate from culture's rapid change and definitive generation gap. Other older women take a retirement mentality, thinking, "I've paid my dues; it's their turn now."[6]

Rewards and Pitfalls

Mentoring relationships between younger and older women can offer many rewards. Older women usually have less outside pressures and more time to interact with younger friends. "Junior buddies" can offer a fresh slant on life. Both young and old can enjoy a daughter/mother/grandmother relationship without the inherent problems – the bond without the baggage. They can offer each other a perspective and depth in conversation that is sometimes lacking with peers.[7]

With all the advantages of mentoring, it does not always come easily. For example, some women do not allow enough time and energy for mentoring. Although it is not necessary to devote inordinate amounts of time and energy, it will take a certain amount of these to make a mentoring relationship work. Each woman should be available whenever she is needed.

Sometimes a mentor assumes that her mentee should be her clone. A mentor serves as an advisor who may recommend or inform, but she should be hesitant to tell her mentee what to do. The mentee is a person in her own right with her own feelings and beliefs. The mentor's goal should be to guide and support, not to manipulate and control.

Occasionally a mentee wants to cling to her mentor for too long. Many mentee/mentor relationships are temporary and meant to cross through a specific stage in their lives, such as becoming a new bride or parenting teenage children. Hopefully, as the mentee grows, she will be better prepared to accomplish what she needs to do. Ideally both women can give each other independence and exit gracefully with gratitude.

How Do You Begin?

If you are interested in being mentored or mentoring, look around. Be on the lookout for someone with whom you would feel comfortable – someone who might be willing to get to know you better in a mentoring relationship. She should have a love for God and for people. [8] She should be someone you can trust implicitly who will not share your secret fears and burning questions with anyone (even her husband!). It is paramount that mentees be willing enough to ask and mentors be available to serve. Pray about finding the right person.[9]

Some women just ask someone to mentor them. To match up those who are seeking mentors, some congregations offer programs as well as suggestions for resources. Other women find organized mentoring groups beneficial, based on a common need such as living a single fulfilling life, building stronger marriages or surviving children from the "booties to braces" years. They have found that these groups not only encourage Christian women but also serve as a valuable outreach to outsiders.[10] Decide what your purpose will be. Each relationship is looking for something different, and it is up to those involved to decide what that will be. Focus on what you both can share and contribute, whether it is studying the Bible, spending time together, discussing a book together, or holding each other accountable for problem areas in your lives.[11] For example, your situation might call for mentoring in teaching. Perhaps you might sit in and observe your mentor as she teaches a Bible class. Next, she encourages you to co-teach with her. Then you teach a lesson by yourself, asking her for input. Finally you start teaching on your own. From the perspective of the mentor, the process might go like this: "I do, you watch. I do, you help. You do, I help. You do, I watch."[12]

Be creative in finding ways to get together. Enjoy whatever you can do together – walking, cooking, quilting, running or gardening. Meet for coffee, make a lunch date, or take afternoon tea. Mentoring is spending time building relationships.[13]

You've Got Mail

Many Christian women have found the Internet to be a timesaving and beneficial way to mentor one-on-one or as a group. With the capability of instant messaging, blogs and social networking websites such as Facebook, mentors and mentees can keep in touch in real time. Others have found the convenience and speed of e-mail perfect for their busy schedules.

For example, the Harding Sisters Network serves as a resource for mentoring a group of women all over the world. This service is sponsored by the Harding University Marriage and Family Therapy Department, and there is no cost involved to subscribers. A woman on the Harding University campus serves as a moderator for the e-mail list. She screens all mail and sends it out to any woman who asks to be included on the list. If someone on the list has a prayer request, question, suggestion or problem, she e-mails the moderator and the moderator sends it to the group. A subscriber may reply if she wishes. She may also remain anonymous to the group if she chooses. Such varied topics as dealing with grief and loneliness, reaching an unbelieving husband, getting out of debt, and rejuvenating church ladies activities have been discussed. A valuable sense of sharing and support is provided through this list.

This e-mail mentoring idea could be modified to meet the needs of ladies in a congregation or in congregations in a city or region. Another variation on this theme is for several older women in a congregation to write articles that are e-mailed to younger women. These articles could serve as a source of encouragement to all the ladies in the group.[14]

Mary and Elizabeth would laugh to see all the sophisticated ways in which women can mentor each other now. For them, it was simply being there together, sharing their lives. That is really the essence of what we need to give each other as women – simply being there for each other. Mary Farrar put it well: "Just as survivalists need each other in the wilderness, so we desperately need the input and support of one another on the trail of biblical womanhood."[15] With the Lord's help and each other, we can make it through the jungle – alive and well and together.

Searching Further

1. Under what circumstances could a woman be stoned (Deuteronomy 22:23-29)? Why was there a difference in sentence between the location of town and country?

2. According to the terms of a betrothal, why did Joseph have the right to divorce Mary? Why did he not choose this option (Matthew 1:18-25)?

3. What did Elizabeth and Mary have in common? How were they different? What made theirs a supportive mentoring relationship?

4. What was Elizabeth's attitude when she greeted Mary? What did Elizabeth's baby do when Mary appeared (Luke 1:39-45)?

5. At least how many children did Mary have (Matthew 13:55-56)?

6. What did Paul write Titus to teach the older women? What should older women then teach younger women (Titus 2:3-5)?

7. What are some reasons we might not mentor each other more? What are some advantages of mentoring? What are some pitfalls?

8. What are some qualities to look for in a mentor?

9. What are some ways congregations can help women in the mentoring process?

10. How can the Internet be utilized effectively in mentoring women?

Who Else?

Who else probably served as a spiritual mentor to a younger woman (2 Timothy 1:5)?

Safari Savvy
Do It Now!

Friendship is dynamic. It doesn't stay the same because we don't stay the same. It is in constant change, just like a buoy on the ocean. Sometimes it remains steady, even with the relentless pounding of the waves. Other times it drifts away for lack of mooring.

Sometimes we unintentionally let our friendships drift away. We forget how precious they are. We need to remember Proverbs 3:27-28: "Do not withhold good from those who deserve it, when it is in your power to act. Do not say to your neighbor, 'Come back later; I'll give it tomorrow' – when you now have it with you."

If you can do something to show your love to your friend, do it today. If a friend needs your listening ear, she probably needs it now, not tomorrow when another stress has been added to the last one. If you can show your appreciation to her for all she has done, thank her now. If you can surprise her with her favorite flower or hand lotion or novel, do not stop until you see the joy in her face! If you can congratulate her when she has done well, applaud her now. If you can encourage her when she is disheartened, lift her up now. If you can inspire her to keep going, do not wait – do it now.

The moment may pass. A hundred things may come up to distract you from your good intentions. You may get involved in something else you consider important. You may move. She may move. You may grow distant from the busyness of life. She may die in an accident, or you might. You may never get to tell her or show her or surprise her.

Do not let the opportunity fly by.

Do it now.

Reviewing Your Trip:
Mining Jungle Gems

I f you are searching for practical advice for personal relationships, look no further than the book of Proverbs. It is a collection of gems of wisdom written by none other than the wisest man who ever lived, Solomon, and his fellow sages. This book is a compilation of pithy sayings and thought-provoking insights for getting along with people, especially other women. Although these principles are ancient, they are amazingly relevant today in our sleek techno-culture. Solomon's divine gift of wisdom coupled with his keen observation of people make him a counselor worth heeding. Who knows how many gems Solomon mined from his own experience with the women in his palace? After all, he had a total of 700 wives and 300 concubines (1 Kings 11:3)!

How could the following verses in Proverbs apply to various Bible characters in our study on women's relationships? How could they apply to your daily life in the jungle? Mine the Jungle Gems from Proverbs and find out! (The first example has been done for you.)

In a class setting, make this a fun activity by hosting a carry-in meal to close out the study. What better way to enrich friendships! The teacher chooses several proverbs that could be easily performed and divides the class into teams. Each team acts out several proverbs, and the other teams must guess what they represent. The team with the most points gets to eat first!

• **How can I be a better friend?** Proverbs 10:12 states, "Hatred stirs up dissension, but love covers over all wrongs." Joseph's brothers hated him, but his love "covered" their wrongs in forgiveness. In the same way, some women may hate us, but we are called to love and forgive them. Even when our friends may occasionally wrong us, it is better to cover over their faults with love and forgiveness.

Proverbs 15:30   Proverbs 17:17
Proverbs 18:24   Proverbs 25:17
Proverbs 27:9   Proverbs 27:10

• **What "mouth traps" should I avoid to have better friendships?**
Proverbs 12:18   Proverbs 16:28
Proverbs 17:9   Proverbs 17:14
Proverbs 18:13   Proverbs 22:24-25
Proverbs 25:9-10

• **How can my words enrich my friendships?**
Proverbs 12:25   Proverbs 15:1
Proverbs 15:4   Proverbs 15:23
Proverbs 16:24   Proverbs 25:11
Proverbs 25:12   Proverbs 27:6

• **How did some men in our study prove the truth of these proverbs?**
Proverbs 10:27   Proverbs 15:18
Proverbs 16:18   Proverbs 18:12

• **How did some women in our study prove the truth of these proverbs?**
Proverbs 11:7   Proverbs 11:16
Proverbs 14:30   Proverbs 15:13

Endnotes

Introduction — *The Way of the Jungle*

1. Bob Phillips, *Phillips' Book of Great Thoughts and Funny Sayings* (Wheaton, Ill.: Tyndale House, 1993) 111.

Chapter 1 — *She's Meaner Than a Snake*

1. Leslie A. Burton, Jessica Hafetz and Debra Henninger, "Gender Differences in Relational and Physical Aggression," *Social Behavior and Personality* 35.1 (2007): 42.

2. Cheryl Dellasega, *Mean Girls Grown Up: Adult Women Who Are Still Queen Bees, Middle Bees, and Afraid-to-Bees* (Hoboken, N.J.: John Wiley & Sons, 2005) 10-11.

3. Pat Heim, Susan A. Murphy and Susan K. Golant, *In the Company of Women: Indirect Aggression Among Women: Why We Hurt Each Other and How to Stop* (New York: Jeremy P. Tarcher/Putnam, 2001) 6-7.

4. Heim 9.

5. Heim 9.

6. Margaret Talbot, "Girls Just Want to Be Mean," *New York Times Magazine* 24 Feb. 2002: 26.

7. Kenneth L. Barker and John Kohlenberger III, eds., *Zondervan NIV Bible Commentary, Volume 1: Old Testament* (Grand Rapids, Mich.: Zondervan, 1994) 198.

8. Dellasega 12.

9. Dellasega 12-13.

10. Rusty Wright and Linda Raney Wright, *500 Clean Jokes and Humorous Stories and How to Tell Them* (Ulrichsville, Ohio: Barbour Publishing, 1985) 52.

11. Adapted from Edwin Markham. "Outwitted." *The Shoes of Happiness and Other Poems* (Garden City, N.Y.: Doubleday, Page and Company, 1915) 1.

12. Laurence J. Peter, *Peter's Quotations: Ideas for Our Time* (New York: Bantam, 1989) 419.

13. Marla Paul, *The Friendship Crisis: Finding, Making, and Keeping Friends When You're Not a Kid Anymore* (Emmaus, Pa.: Rodale, 2005) 17, 82-83.

Chapter 2 – Me Tarzan, You Jane

1. Joyce F. Benenson and Athena Christakos, "The Greater Fragility of Females' Versus Males' Closest Same-Sex Friendships," *Child Development* July/Aug. 2003: 1123.

2. Nan Mooney, *I Can't Believe She Did That!: Why Women Betray Other Women at Work* (New York: St. Martin's Press, 2005) 52.

3. Mooney 54.

4. Heim 5-6.

5. Lauren Duncan and Ashli Owen-Smith, "Powerlessness and the Use of Indirect Aggression in Friendships," *Sex Roles* 55 (2006): 493-494.

6. Heim 108-109.

7. Mooney 5.

8. Mooney 5.

9. Mooney 5.

10. Heim 111.

11. "About Relational Aggression," *It Takes a Girl to Change the World* 24 July 2007 <http://ittakesagirl.com/ra.html>.

12. Judith Selee McClure, *Civilized Assertiveness for Women: Communication With Backbone … Not Bite* (Denver: Albion Street Press, 2003) 44.

13. Julia Balzer Riley, *Communication in Nursing* (St. Louis: Mosby, 1996) 8.

14. Ruth N. Koch and Kenneth C. Haugk, *Speaking the Truth in Love: How to Be an Assertive Christian* (St. Louis: Stephen Ministries, 1992) 23-25.

15. Koch 23-24.

16. Koch 61-66.

17. Meda Chesney-Lind, "The Meaning of Mean," *The Women's Review of Books* Nov. 2002: 22. Retrieved 28 Jan. 2007 from Academic Search Premier database (Document ID: 7585033).

18. Duncan 498.

19. Paul 153-155.

Chapter 3 - Monkey See, Monkey Do

1. Solly Zuckerman, *The Social Life of Monkeys and Apes* (London: Routledge, 1999) 166.

2. Craig S. Keener, *The IVP Bible Background Commentary: New Testament* (Downers Grove, Ill.: InterVarsity Press, 1993) 150.

3. Keener 151.

4. William Barclay, *The Gospel of Mark* (Philadelphia: Westminster Press, 1975) 150.

5. Barclay, *Mark* 152.

6. Earle McMillan, *The Gospel According to Mark* (Austin: Sweet, 1973) 81-82.

7. Keener 150-151.

8. Susan Shapiro Barash, *Tripping the Prom Queen: The Truth About Women and Rivalry* (New York: St. Martin's Griffin, 2006) 49.

9. Mooney 4.

10. "Understanding Mother-Daughter Relationships," *USA Today Magazine* May 2001: 9. Retrieved 14 March 2008 from Academic Search Premier database (Document ID: 4393345).

11. Mooney 4.

12. Katherine Marsh, "Can Your Mom Be Your Best Friend?" *Good Housekeeping* May 2000: 98.

13. Marsh 98.

14. Birdie Lee Etchison, "Love Your Daughter as Your Neighbor," *Christian Woman* May/June 1994: 16.

15. Mary Farrar, *Choices: For Women Who Long to Discover Life's Best* (Sisters, Ore.: Multnomah Books, 1994) 153.

16. Carmen Renee Berry and Tamara Traeder, *Girlfriends: Invisible Bonds, Enduring Ties* (Berkeley, Calif.: Wildcat Canyon Press, 1995) 90.

17. Jane McWhorter, *Friendship: Handle With Care* (Nashville, Tenn.: Gospel Advocate, 1999) 77.

Chapter 4 – Don't Leave Home Without It

1. John H. Walton, Victor H. Matthews and Mark Chavalas, *The IVP Bible Background Commentary: Old Testament* (Downers Grove, Ill.: InterVarsity Press, 2000) 390.

2. Tonya Fischio, "Mean Girls Start in Preschool," *Marriage and Families* Winter 2006: 28.

3. "Children Changing Lives: Another Birthday Bash Hosted for HHI," *Healing Hands International News* 3 (2007): 2.

4. "Children Changing Lives: Teen Takes Initiative," *Healing Hands International News* 3 (2007): 2.

5. "Quotations About Kindness," *Quotegarden.com* 2 Nov. 2007 <http://www.quotegarden.com/kindness.html>.

6. Vern McLellan, *Shredded Wit* (Eugene, Ore.: Harvest House, 1988) 19.

7. "Plato Quotes," *Famous Inspirational Quotes* 24 July 2008 <http://www.inspirationalquotes4u.com/platoquotes/index.html>.

8. Dellasega 204-205.

Chapter 5 – Queen of the Jungle

1. "Lion Facts," *Barbarylion.com* 28 May 2008 <http://www.barbarylion.com/Facts.htm>.

2. Dellasega 2.

3. W. Shaw Caldecott and David F. Payne, "Athalia," *International Standard Bible Encyclopedia*, Vol. 1, A-D (Grand Rapids: Eerdmans, 1979) 349.

4. Caldecott 349.

5. Dellasega 39.

6. Stacie Dilts-Harryman, "When Bullies Grow Up," *ASCA School Counselor* Nov./Dec. 2004:29.

7. "Bullying – For Girls," *girlshealth.gov* 14 Sept 2007 <http://www.girlshealth.gov/bullying/whybully.htm>.

8. Dellasega 36.

9. Anita Bruzzese, "Get Rid of Bullies in the Workplace, *USAToday.com* 12 Nov. 2002. 28 March 2007 <http:www.usatoday.com/money/jobcenter/workplace/relationships/2002-11-12-bullies_x.htm?POE=Click-refer>.

10. Dilts-Harryman 30.

11. Dilts-Harryman 30.

12. Lisa Stone, "What Do You Do When You're Cyberstalked, Taunted or Abused Online?" *BlogHer* 31 Oct. 2006. 3 May 2007 <http://blogher.org/node/12104>.

13. Dilts-Harryman 30.

14. Dellasega 37.

15. Stone.

16. Melissa Breazile-Ensz, "When Bullies Grow Up: Workplace Bullying" *Today's Omaha Woman* Feb. 2005: 10.

17. Dilts-Harryman 31.

18. Bruzzese.

19. Liz Welch, "Friends in Need," *Real Simple* Oct. 2006: 109-110, 112, 114, 116.

Chapter 6 – Blabbermouth Birds

1. "Roman Life Expectancy" 3 Nov. 2007 <http//www.utexas.edu/depts/classics/documents/Life.html>.

2. William Barclay, *The Letters to Timothy, Titus and Philemon* (Philadelphia: Westminster Press, 1975) 114.

3. Carl Spain, *The Letters of Paul to Timothy and Titus* (Abilene: ACU Press, 1984) 85-87.

4. Arlan J. Birkey, "Gossip," *International Standard Bible Encyclopedia*, Vol. 2, E-J (Grand Rapids, Mich.: Eerdmans, 1982) 536.

5. Spiros Zodhiates, ed., *Hebrew-Greek Key Word Study Bible, New International Version* (Chattanooga, Tenn.: AMG Publishers, 1996) 1688.

6. Heim 116.

7. Barker, *Old Testament* 977.

8. F.F. Bruce, ed., *International Bible Commentary With the New International Version* (Grand Rapids, Mich.: Zondervan, 1986) 674.

9. Heim 118.

10. Charlie T. Jones and Bob Phillips, *Wit and Wisdom* (Eugene, Ore.: Harvest House, 1977) 125.

11. "Quotations About Gossip" 2 Nov. 2007 <http://www.quotegarden.com/gossip.html>.

12. James S. Hewett, ed., *Illustrations Unlimited* (Wheaton, Ill.: Tyndale House, 1988) 474.

13. Hewett 476.

14. McLellan 81.

15. Sheri Rose Shepherd, *Fit for Excellence* (Orlando, Fla.: Creation House, 1998) 136-137.

16. "How Did Jesus Use Humor to Teach About God? What Was Jesus' Sense of Humor?" 9 Nov. 2007 <http://www.biblestudy.org/basicart/how-did-jesus-use-humor-to-teach-about-god.html>.

17. McLellan 109.

18. Berry 208-210.

19. Berry 211.

Chapter 7 – Target Practice

1. Walton 281.

2. Walton 281-282.

3. Dellasega 122.

4. Dellasega 124.

5. Dellasega 124-125.

6. Dianna Booher, *10 Smart Moves for Women Who Want to Succeed in Love and Life* (Tulsa, Okla.: Trade Life Books, 1997) 101-117.

7. "Ruth Graham," *Answers.com* 2 Oct. 2007 <http://www.answers.com/topic/ruth-graham>.

Chapter 8 – Hiding Behind the Ferns

1. Kenneth L. Barker and John R. Kohlenberger III, eds., *Zondervan NIV Bible Commentary, Volume 2: New Testament* (Grand Rapids, Mich.: Zondervan, 1994) 808.

2. Heim 212-213.

3. Heim 220.

4. Heim 212-213.

5. Heim 224.

6. Heim 224.

7. Heim 222-223.

8. Heim 223.

9. Heim 225-226.

10. Heim 226-227.

11. Heim 227-228.

12. Walton 325-326.

13. Heim 220-222.

14. Phillips 137.

15. Heim 188, 197-199.

16. Dellasega 230.

17. Ann Hibbard, *Treasured Friends: Finding and Keeping True Friendships* (Grand Rapids, Mich.: Baker Books, 2004) 153.

Chapter 9 – Getting Ahead, Falling Behind

1. Derek Kidner, *Genesis: An Introduction and Commentary* (Downers Grove, Ill.: InterVarsity Press, 1967) 160.

2. John T. Willis, *Genesis* (Abilene, Texas: ACU Press, 1984) 337.

3. Walton 61.

4. Willis 338.

5. Willis 342.

6. Jan Yager, *When Friendship Hurts: How to Deal With Friends Who Betray, Abandon, or Wound You* (New York: Simon & Schuster, 2002) 106.

7. Berry 169.

8. Paul 146-150.

Chapter 10 – Hanging on for Dear Life

1. D. Guthrie, J.A. Motyer and A.M. Stibbs, eds., *The New Bible Commentary Revised* (Grand Rapids, Mich.: Eerdmans, 1970) 280.

2. Walton 277.

3. Barker, *Old Testament* 371.

4. Walton 277.

5. Walton 278.

6. Guthrie 280.

7. Barker, *Old Testament* 371.

8. Barker, *Old Testament* 369.

9. Guthrie 280.

10. Barker, *Old Testament* 376.

11. William Barclay, *New Testament Words* (Louisville, Ky.: Westminster John Knox Press, 1974) 245-247.

12. Marion Leach Jacobsen, *Crowded Pews and Lonely People* (Wheaton, Ill.: Tyndale House, 1976) 81-82.

13. "Tips of the Week: At Work," *Words Can Heal* 4 Nov. 2007 <http://www.wordscanheal.org/newsletter/tip_of_week_at_work.htm>.

14. Booher 144.

15. Hibbard 136.

16. Paul 166-169.

Chapter 11 – Playing Games of Power

1. Walton 48.

2. Kidner 126.

3. Willis 240.

4. Leora Tanenbaum, *Catfight: Rivalries Among Women – From Diets to Dating, From the Boardroom to the Delivery Room* (New York: HarperCollins, 2003) 176-177.

5. Institute for Management Excellence, "Online Newsletter: Bullying in the Workplace," July 2005. 14 Sept. 2007 <http://www.itstime.com/print/jul2005p.htm>.

6. Zodhiates 1571.

7. Dellasega 224.

Chapter 12 – Yodeling and Other Jungle Communication

1. H. Norman Wright, *Communication @ Work* (Ventura, Calif.: Regal Books, 2001) 28.

2. McLellan 110.

3. Wright 85-86.

4. McClure 51.

5. McClure 52, 74.

6. McClure 84.

7. McClure 84-85.

8. McClure 85-86.

9. McClure 123.

10. McClure 124-126.

11. Kristyn Kusek Lewis, "18 Common Phrases to Avoid in Conversation," *Real Simple* Nov. 2007. 7 July 2008 <http://www.realsimple.com/realsimple/gallery/0,21863,1698308,00.html>.

12. Dellasega 229.

13. Lewis.

Chapter 13 – Following Your Guide

1. Keener 190.

2. Anthony Lee Ash, *The Gospel According to Luke: Part 1, 1:1–9:50* (Austin, Texas: Sweet, 1975) 40.

3. Ash 35.

4. Keener 190.

5. Paul 185.

6. Farrar 152.

7. Paul 189, 191-192.

8. Kelley Mathews, "How Christian Women Can Mentor and Be Mentored," *Crosswalk* 24 Nov. 2007 <http://www.crosswalk.com/1409871/page1/>.

9. Ruthann Raycroft, "Mentoring From Your Computer: What Is a Good Mentor?" *Christian Women Today* 24 Nov. 2007 <http://christianwomen today.com/growth/mentoring.html>.

10. Linda Parker, "A Ministry of Mentoring," *Christian Woman* March/Apr. 2007: 16.

11. Raycroft.

12. Mathews.

13. Mathews.

14. Marion Lorence, "mentoring.com: Using the Internet to Connect Today's Busy Women in Your Church," *Just Between Us* 24 Nov. 2007 <http://www.justbetweenus.org/5_04/mentoring.html>.

15. Farrar 154.